KU-181-600

6 00 109621 0

Students and External ch

DATE

Basic needs, poverty and
government policies in Sri Lanka

UNIVERSITY LIBRARY

11 AUG 1980

NOTTINGHAM

Basic needs, poverty and government policies in Sri Lanka

Peter Richards and Wilbert Gooneratne

International Labour Office   Geneva

Copyright © International Labour Organisation 1980

Publications of the International Labour Office enjoy copyright under Protocol 2 of the Universal Copyright Convention. Nevertheless, short excerpts from them may be reproduced without authorisation, on condition that the source is indicated. For rights of reproduction or translation, application should be made to the Editorial and Translation Branch, International Labour Office, CH-1211 Geneva 22, Switzerland. The International Labour Office welcomes such applications.

ISBN 92-2-102316-8

First published 1980

The designations employed in ILO publications, which are in conformity with United Nations practice, and the presentation of material therein do not imply the expression of any opinion whatsoever on the part of the International Labour Office concerning the legal status of any country or territory or of its authorities, or concerning the delimitation of its frontiers.
The responsibility for opinions expressed in signed articles, studies and other contributions rests solely with their authors, and publication does not constitute an endorsement by the International Labour Office of the opinions expressed in them.

ILO publications can be obtained through major booksellers or ILO local offices in many countries, or direct from ILO Publications, International Labour Office, CH-1211 Geneva 22, Switzerland. A catalogue or list of new publications will be sent free of charge from the above address.

Printed by the International Labour Office, Geneva, Switzerland

Acknowledgements

The authors would like to thank S.M.P. Senanayake and P.J. Gunewardane of the Agrarian Research and Training Institute, Colombo, for their assistance in data collection.

TABLE OF CONTENTS

In 1976 the World Employment Conference of the International Labour Organisation adopted a Declaration of Principles and Programme of Action enshrining the promotion of employment and the satisfaction of basic needs. The concept of basic needs, however, remains country-specific. Different nations can lay emphasis on different aspects. Sri Lanka has for many years pursued welfare policies which have distributed health care, education and subsidised food to rich and poor alike. However, side by side with these welfare policies have gone a slow rate of economic growth and an alarmingly high rate of unemployment. This juxtaposition has often created the suspicion that welfare policies and fast growth are incompatible, that the one starves the other of funds or sets up a perverse system of incentives.

In this study, the authors, Peter Richards of the ILO and Wilbert Gooneratne of the Agrarian Research and Training Institute in Colombo, Sri Lanka, find the arguments for a trade-off between welfare and growth unconvincing. Welfare policies had some negative and some positive effects on growth and employment. But of more importance in explaining Sri Lanka's performance have been various factors peculiar to the country. Welfare policies served to bring about a compromise between the conflicting interests of various groups in society and allowed traditional relationships, above all in rural areas, to continue unchanged. Slow growth, on the other hand, could be traced back to a misplaced choice of policies, such as a preference for import substitution and for controls in the face of foreign exchange restriction, over exports. Similarly agricultural investment policy has favoured the development of large-scale and low-yielding irrigation schemes over, administratively more difficult, small-scale labour-intensive land development. The extensive private plantation sector failed to re-invest and raise its productivity, in the expectation of nationalisation, and failed to stimulate alternative export products.

This study was undertaken within the framework of the Income Distribution and Employment Programme of the WEP. Within this programme, a number of studies are being undertaken in different parts of the world aiming at the elucidation of various issues concerned with different types of income distribution and at exploring the relationship between income distribution and employment. This programme is also concerned with the instruments of government redistribution policy, such as government expenditure and taxation, with the area of wealth distribution and redistribution and with the problem of poverty and the satisfaction of basic needs.

A relatively recent emphasis of the Income Distribution and Employment Programme has been on the role of government services in the satisfaction of basic needs. The study by Peter Richards and Wilbert Gooneratne represents the first systematic effort to investigate the impact of government policies on the satisfaction of basic needs and the alleviation of poverty in Sri Lanka.

Felix Paukert,
Chief,
Income Distribution
and International Employment
Policies Branch

CHAPTER 1

Introduction

The Programme of Action of the World Employment Conference[1] spoke of basic needs in the following terms, "certain minimum requirements of a family for private consumption: adequate food, shelter and clothing ... second ... essential services provided by and for the community at large, such as safe drinking water, sanitation, public transport and health, educational and cultural facilities. A basic-needs-oriented policy implies the participation of the people in making the decisions which affect them through organisations of their own choice. In all countries freely chosen employment enters into a basic-needs policy both as a means and as an end ... . It is important to recognise that the concept of basic needs is a country specific and dynamic concept ... . In no circumstances should it be taken to mean merely the minimum necessary for subsistence ... ."

The Programme continues, "In developing countries satisfaction of basic needs cannot be achieved without both acceleration in their economic growth and measures aimed at changing the pattern of growth and access to the use of resources by the lowest income groups. Often these measures will require the transformation of social structures, including an initial redistribution of assets, especially land, with adequate and timely compensation."

The two preceding paragraphs give the bare bones of what is meant by a basic needs strategy or by basic needs satisfaction. How does Sri Lanka fit this outline? In terms of its output of goods and services for personal enjoyment the country is obviously poor. In 1977 annual per capita private consumption amounted to some Rs 1,600 (or the equivalent of a week's stay in a tourist hotel) so that the amount of goods and services which can be supplied by the current production capacity of the economy is limited. Sri Lanka is a country with a widespread transport and distribution network so that one major obstacle to achieving a fairly similar level of enjoyment of basic consumption needs throughout the country is removed. Local variations are also likely to be minimised by the presence of a relatively centralised administrative system which, conversely, may reduce the scale of local participation in many administrative and investment decisions. Ethnically and socially as we shall see it is a country which

---

[1] Quotations from paras. 1-6 of the Programme of Action from the Declaration of Principles and Programme of Action of the World Employment Conference, ILO, Geneva, 1976.

is not so homogenous that elements of conflict and exploitation may not
appear. It has an economy where, now, either small scale production units
based on the household, with some wage labour, or government run enterprises predominate. As a result many forces working towards income inequality are weakened, but labour conditions and earnings can vary
substantially and job security is often low. Population pressure on the
land has grown quickly, land ownership is naturally very coveted and as a
result fragmentation, part-time farming and, possibly, tenancy have
increased.

Sri Lanka is furthermore a country where many welfare state measures
have been in operation for a long period. Relatively high standards of
health, and a high level of life expectancy, have been reached by centrally
controlled mass environmental health measures and by a wide coverage of
government personal health services. Education programmes have expanded
fast, except at the university level where elitism has prevailed; but the
expansion of even primary education may have run up against "natural"
obstacles of poverty, disinterest and inconvenience (the last particularly
in sparsely populated areas). Food subsidies have provided an over-all
income supplement which is, almost certainly, a major and unusual element
in the working of such an economy. Food subsidies have contributed to
the absence of large-scale food shortages, although given the climate of
Sri Lanka and some elements of distributional justice, these would be
unlikely. Domestic food production has increased, although never fast
enough to remove the need for a high level of imports. The distributive
consequences of the means used to raise domestic agricultural output form
one of the chapters of this study.

Sri Lanka was famous as a country extremely dependent on foreign
trade. Import substitution has obviously taken place on a large scale
over the past 20 years but imports of machinery, many industrial raw
materials, above all of textiles and of food,[1] still continue. No doubt,
there is a sense in which the country could manage with a lower level of
food imports; consumption could switch to many more basic substitutes of
rice or of wheat; but consumption habits are hard to change. Furthermore,

---

[1] While rice production grew at some 3 per cent p.a. from 1952-1976
the share of imports in total cereal consumption fell only from slightly
above to slightly below 50 per cent.

if there was such a switch, the level of consumption of such items as
manioc would be an undesirably conspicuous mark of poverty. On the
export side the purchasing power of the old staples, tea, rubber and
coconut, has conspicuously fallen, while the traditional trading system
has failed to find new sources of foreign exchange sufficient even to give
a breathing space. This was, in a way, inevitable; the old London links
of the estate companies were interested in getting money out of, not into,
Sri Lanka, while the machinery of government has proved inflexible and
anyway inward-looking.

The ILO's Programme of Action also stresses the need for the "participation of the people in making the decisions which affect them." There is
no doubt, however, in Sri Lanka, that certain groups participate more than
others. The prime example, of course, is the disenfranchisement of the
bulk of estate workers after Independence. Nevertheless they have and
had the largest trade unions in the country, which represent them at wages
board meetings and other negotiations. Sri Lanka citizens, of course, have
the right to vote, which they use most effectively to dismiss unpopular
Governments. They vote in national elections, in village council, town
council and municipal elections, in rural development societies, in co-
operative societies, in temple committees or in parent teachers' organisations. Nevertheless, whenever these organisations have any real power
to wield the richer and more influential groups would appear to control
them. Thus when cultivation committees were elective (and not nominated)
they were generally ineffective in protecting the interests of tenants
because of dominance by the major farmers.

While there are certain ways in which Sri Lanka seems to fit well
into the basic needs outline, particularly through its welfare provisions
and through its generally democratic political system, three opposing
factors can be identified. These are the low over-all level of economic
growth, the extent of unemployment and the perpetuation of poverty together
with insecurity.

One basic point is that the best estimate of real income growth in
Sri Lanka from 1953 to 1976 was a maximum of 1 per cent p.a. per capita;
the actual figure may have been slightly lower (population growth was some
2.3 per cent, total real income growth was some 3.3 per cent).[1] The growth
of per capita GNP was higher but there were major losses through the adverse
external terms of trade. There was nevertheless some structural shift in

---

[1] For a general description of Sri Lanka's economic development until
the late 1960s, see H.N.S. Karunatilleka, Economic development in Ceylon,
Praeger, 1971.

GNP with agriculture falling by some 6 percentage points and the share of manufacturing in non-agriculture doubling. Manufacturing growth was aided by the very considerable degree of import substitution which took place over this period: at 1959 prices imports fell from nearly 30 per cent of GNP in 1953 to some 10 per cent in 1976. Nevertheless the over-all rate of growth of output has been extremely disappointing taken over a long period.

The Programme of Action implies that unemployment is the denial of a basic need for a feeling of self-respect and dignity. If this is so then Sri Lanka's position with, in the late 1970s, probably around one million unemployed in a population of some 14 million is a sorry one.[1] Wide-scale unemployment has been endemic in Sri Lanka over the last 20 years, a fact which may have led some observers to link its prevalence to the implementation of welfare policies. But to discuss unemployment per se, without analysing its consequences for the young and the old or the rich and the poor, is to over-simplify drastically. If unemployment is a cost involved in achieving other welfare targets then it is a cost whose incidence is borne differently. Conversely unemployment may be largely a result of the very slowly changing over-all economic structure. We will return to the subject in later chapters.

That poverty should be perpetuated under conditions of very low per capita income growth may not seem surprising. But poverty in the sense of low incomes and levels of consumption is associated also with job insecurity and, in rural areas, landlessness and disguised tenancy. As we shall see later some of these other poverty characteristics may be intensifying.

We can appreciate the situation of Sri Lanka a little more by viewing it as an archetypal "soft state". To quote G. Myrdal[2] referring to South Asia in general, "These countries are all 'soft states' both in that policies decided on are often not enforced ... and in that the authorities ... are reluctant to place obligations on people. This reluctance, which

---

[1] The income support scheme for the unemployed introduced in mid-1978 covers under 400,000 people. It excludes those under 18, non-citizens, married persons and those from families with a total income of over Rs 500 p.m., see Ministry of Plan Implementation, Employment Data Bank and Income Support Scheme, Colombo, 1979.

[2] G. Myrdal, Asian Drama, London, 1968.

derives from the economic, social and political structure ... is then
excused and indeed idealized ... ." The characteristic of a "soft
state" has at least two correlates: apparently greater government
tendency to give in than to give orders and a propensity towards
"unresolved compromise", in Gold's words.[1]

That countries should run systems of universal education and
effective health care does not necessarily make them "soft states".
However, that Sri Lanka should apparently subsidise both food consumption
(the rice ration) and food production (the Guaranteed Price Scheme, GPS)
and more recently introduce an income support scheme for the unemployed[2]
might seem excessive pampering. We shall pour some cold water on this
apparent extravagance below; thus some foods were in fact sold at a considerable profit while GPS prices were usually below a realistic import
price. However, these must be seen as populist measures and indeed until
1978 they were not even restricted to the identifiably poorer groups.
(In late 1977 subsidised food was restricted to the poorest 50 per cent
of the population.) Side by side with this "welfarism" has gone e.g. the
unwillingness or inability to collect various acreage levies for irrigation
and to impose necessary discipline in the use of irrigation water. However,
it must be pointed out that in general taxes have been collected with what
would seem a reasonable degree of social discipline.

The "unresolved compromise" to which Gold refers specifically is the
Paddy Lands Act of 1958 which we shall review in detail in Chapter 6.
For him this represents an "incremental approach" to social reform where
radical and conservative forces can both be satisfied. To quote Gold,
"the reformers will point to the changes in ideals as embodied in the
substantive parts of the new law, while the traditional leadership will
remain confident that the law is basically unenforceable." However, such
a compromise is not necessarily the triumph of cynicism, it may, as Gold
points out, "reflect an appreciation of the depth of the problem and the
difficulty of changing norms, systems and relationships that are ingrained

---

[1] M.E. Gold, Law and Scoial Change, A Study of Land Reform in Sri
Lanka, New York, 1977.

[2] Introduced in 1978, this gives Rs 50 p.m. subject to certain
qualifications.

by generations and generations of tradition and acceptance."

Cynicism, however, has been a trait that Myrdal perceived in Sri
Lankan politics. He wrote, "Radical nationalism in Ceylon, although
imbued with the vague socialism (S.W.R.D.) Bandaranaike professed, has been
more concerned with jobs than with ideology." And again, "Policies have not
been conceived from a national point of view but only in terms of how they
will affect the interests of a particular group or community." Jiggins[1]
writes that after 1956, "Over the next twenty years MPs have increasingly
expressed their role as largely, if not wholly, relating to the satisfaction of their supporters' demands, the solution of their problems with
the bureaucracy by personal intervention and the securing of tangible benefits for their constituencies." (We shall revert to this general topic
when we discuss participation in Chapter 8.) Perhaps it can be argued that
parliamentary democracy, plus the perpetuation of some very conservative
traditions plus the open acknowledgement of different group interests leads
inevitably in this direction. It does not, no doubt, satisfy Myrdal's condition for planning for development that, "It requires ... rigorous enforce-
ment of obligations, in which compulsion plays a strategic role."[2] However,
it may be realistic given the awareness of different group interests and
an aversion to open confrontation.

In Sri Lanka there are, as in any society, group differences and interests
and group loyalties. Some of these interests and loyalties overlap, such
that e.g. class interests or religious interests may bind together different
ethnic or caste groups. Other interests may, however, be only further
sources and refinements of division. Furthermore the importance of different interests rises and falls. Christian-Buddhist differences may well
be less important now than they were earlier in the century. Sinhalese-
Tamil differences may well be increasing. Class differences and interests
are no doubt increasingly recognised and built upon, although much less in
rural than in urban areas. Caste differences, however, are enduring and
pervasive.

The late 1950s, which probably saw the supremacy of Buddhist over
Christian interests with the schools take-over and of local over Westernised

---

[1] J. Jiggins, Caste and Family in the Politics of the Sinhalese, 1947-1976,
Cambridge University Press, 1979.

[2] G. Myrdal, op. cit.

interests with the Sinhala only movement, also set in motion a worsening of Sinhalese-Tamil relations. Nationalism and to some extent conservatism triumphed when the Indian Tamil planation workers were disenfranchised after Independence. But only later did the indigenous Tamil population (amounting to about 15 per cent of the Sinhalese population) feel threatened by the spread of irrigation and colonisation schemes in Eastern Sri Lanka and by attempts to impose the use of Sinhalese in all districts.[1] The latter did not succeed and Tamil remains a language of instruction and official communication. However, to take an example from higher education, the share of Tamil entrants in science-oriented courses fell from 35 per cent in 1970 to some 15 per cent in 1978.[2] This was brought about deliberately by media standardisation[3] and by district quotas.

On the class side, the two major political parties, the United National Party and the Sri Lanka Freedom Party, have tried to preserve a multi-class image. S.W.R.D. Bandaranaike's attempts to develop a more radical political instrument in the 1950s are generally accepted to have failed so that in essentials the SLFP has to compromise between conflicting class interests in much the same manner as the UNP. The SLFP has, however, a greater history of coalition with the left parties (which have their rural as well as certain urban worker support) which, of course, has only increased its difficulties in seeking compromise. The left parties themselves, the Communist Party and the LSSP (Lanka Sama-Samaja Party) have considerable official trade union support (and therefore at least a nuisance value in the modern and public sectors) and a rural radical and to some extent low caste support. However, the 1971 insurgency of the JVP (Janatha Vimukthi Peramuna) took the leadership of the left parties (then part of the ruling coalition) by surprise.

The insurgency has been ascribed persuasively to caste interests, through an alliance of the very small but educated and socially often well-placed Karava caste with the far larger but very under-represented Batgam and Vahumpara castes. These last two castes contain probably one third of

---

[1] The 1956 Official Language Act was amended in 1958 to allow "reasonable" use of Tamil.

[2] C.R. de Silva, "The Impact of Nationalism on Education" in M. Roberts (ed.), Collective Identities, Nationalisms and Protest in Modern Sri Lanka, Marga, Colombo, 1979.

[3] Ensuring that the share of successful candidates in each medium of instruction was equal to the number attempting the examination.

the Sinhalese population (compared to the major Goyigama caste with probably slightly over half of the Sinhalese population).[1] The general under-representation of these caste groups can be seen from data provided by Jiggins.[2] They have never provided more than 6 per cent of MPs compared to over 60 per cent from the Goyigama caste and in 1971 provided no directors of locally incorporated public companies (while there were very nearly as many Karava as Goyigama listed). Karavas, however, /can share the legitimate low-country complaint that the delimitation of parliamentary electorates overvalues the up-country Kandyan vote.[3]

We do not want to go further into substantive issues in this intro-ductory chapter. The object of this over-all study can be seen as threefold. One object is to review the over-all level of basic needs satisfaction in the country and particularly to look at the operation of welfare programmes. The other objects concern the interaction of different policies and their possible inconsistencies.

On the one side commentaries on Sri Lanka often lay great stress on the possible links between welfare state policies and the country's generally poor growth performance. The links can be postulated to be either through the diversion of investible funds to consumption, or the setting up of perverse incentives, perhaps against food production, perhaps even in favour of unemployment and lengthened job search, at least for those over a certain income level. All these linkages can be debated which, of course, is not to say that the country's growth, export and employment performance could not have been significantly improved by alternative policies. Universal education and a high level of health facilities are however not obviously a barrier to growth in other economies, far from it.

On the other side there is a set of questions to be asked (our third objective) about the interaction of an originally fairly stagnant and conservative rural sector with both this array of welfare state programmes, on the one hand and, on the other hand, a large government input into domestic agricultural programmes. Have these, largely central government

---

[1] Sinhalese are a little over 70 per cent of the total population and some 80 per cent of the voting population.

[2] J. Jiggins, op. cit.

[3] Mainly because the disenfranchised estate population is still counted in fixing electoral boundaries. Electorates are also not to exceed a certain area, which works against the more highly populated regions.

initiated, measures produced very considerable changes in rural areas or has the old structure and the natural forces of population pressure absorbed these new influences and subjected them to their own hierarchical system?

Thus we are asking whether Sri Lanka's approach to a basic needs strategy may not be self-defeating because either it has entailed a reduced rate of economic growth or it has diverted attention from the necessity of undertaking more radical measures to relieve poverty.

The structure of this study is as follows: the first part, which consists of one chapter, reviews a number of indicators of welfare levels. These include calorie intake, educational enrolment, infant mortality and some measures of the adequacy of shelter and of water supplies. We look at these indicators where possible internationally, through time and by district within Sri Lanka. We also review them by income group.

The next part, Chapters 3 and 4, looks into the twin issues of income distribution and poverty. It investigates the current income distribution and reviews a number of major factors related to it, including wage differentials, internal price shifts etc. Under poverty we examine such issues as its relation to hours worked, to unemployment and above all the conditions governing access to land. Parts I and II will therefore help to place the current position of Sri Lanka in a basic needs context.

In the third part (Chapter 5) we present a discussion of certain mainly structural features which must be understood before we can comment on policies. These features include the pattern of government investment, landholding and the falling size of farms, changes in the plantation sector, including the effects of land reform in 1972 and 1975, and changes in the composition of GNP.

In the fourth part we review policies in certain selected fields in more detail. The areas are rural and agricultural policies, particularly affecting small farmers (Chapter 6), policies on participation and decentralised administration (Chapter 7), and education and health policies (Chapter 8). We selected these three areas as those which have the clearest relevance to determining the basic needs satisfaction of the poor.

The final part (Chapter 9) contains the summary and conclusions of the study. Our first objective should be answered as the study progresses. The second and third objectives will be addressed specifically in the conclusions.

PART I: CHAPTER 2
                    Indicators of Welfare Levels

Introduction

In this chapter we look at welfare levels from four different
viewpoints. First of all we compare some aggregate indicators of calorie
consumption, health and school enrolment for Sri Lanka and some other
Asian countries. We also include data on GNP per capita. These indicators generally show Sri Lanka in a favourable position. We next look
at developments in two indicators through time. These are age-specific
death rates and rates of educational enrolment and progression. The
latter suggests that the rate of improvement of this indicator is declining.
Our third comparison is between the various districts of Sri Lanka. This
highlights the relation of a sizeable share of population resident on
estates with higher levels of, in particular, infant mortality. Our
final section then looks at the enjoyment of welfare levels by income group
for each sector, e.g. urban, rural and estate. This allows us to proceed
beyond average levels of various indicators and to understand something of
their distribution.

International comparisons of welfare levels

The relative success of Sri Lanka in achieving high levels of welfare
can be seen from the international comparisons given in Table 1. Sri
Lanka has the lowest (equal with India) level of per capita GNP yet it
has the second highest per capita calorie consumption level and second
lowest infant mortality rate (second in both cases to food-surplus
Thailand) the highest level of life expectancy, the highest incidence of
hospital beds and of primary school (age 6-12) enrolment and the second
highest (after the Philippines) of secondary (age 14-17) enrolment.

Table 1 is, of course, a hotch-potch. It mixes indicators of inputs
(i.e. school enrolment is an input to better education levels) with indicators of outputs. A reduction in infant mortality can be desired for its
own sake and its own contribution to family happiness. Higher life
expectancy has also its intrinsic value, certainly to the extent that
lower mortality is associated with lower morbidity.[1] The incidence of

_____

[1] This has certainly been argued for developed countries, see R.H. Daw,
Journal of the Institute of Actuaries, 1971.

Table 1: Welfare levels in selected Asian countries, early 1970s

Country	GNP per capita[1]	Calories per capita[2]	School enrolment[3] 6-12	School enrolment[3] 14-17	Life expectancy	Infant mortality	Persons per hospital bed
India	150	2,008	53.6	20.2	47.2[4]	122	1,538
Indonesia	180	2,005	n.a.	n.a.	47.5	125	I,452
Philippines	370	2,094	61.6	50.0	60.0	68	785
Sri Lanka	150	2,149	73.4	47.0	65.9	49	330
Thailand	350	2,305	65.4	17.1	57.6[4]	27	1,345

Source: Asian Development Bank, Key Indicators of Developing Countries, October 1976, Vol. VII, No. 2.

[1] US dollars, 1975.

[2] Average 1970-1974.

[3] From UNESCO and national censuses.

[4] Males only.

hospital beds is an input, which may or may not be an essential element in the health production function. The benefits of a high level of secondary school enrolment taken alone are certainly arguable and Sri Lanka's education policy will be discussed later. The level of calories per capita can be seen as both an input (to health) and as an end in itself (i.e. the absence of hunger). GNP per capita is perhaps not even an input, it is rather the promise of inputs in the guise of the sum of available resources.

Let us, for the moment, look a little further into the resources used to achieve these relatively high welfare levels. Calories, of course, represent physical food supplies measured on the basis of their energy providing capacity. Health and education resources can best be measured in financial terms. Although we have already made use of a specific health care indicator in Table 1 (the incidence of hospital beds) such indicators have their drawbacks. They can so easily turn our attention away from non-institutional inputs, such as the books that parents buy for their school-going children, or the use of self-medication. Taking the total of expenditure on resources as a share of GNP allows international comparisons (although unfortunately not for all the same countries as Table 1). These international comparisons will, however, only faithfully reflect "real" resource levels provided firstly that the bulk of these costs are salary costs and secondly that salaries of health and education personnel bear much the same relation to the national average in all countries. If such salaries are relatively low then the same share of GNP buys more resources in terms of man-years. If a significant amount of resources are imported, e.g. drugs, from richer countries then a higher share of GNP is needed in poorer than in richer countries to obtain the same amount of resources.

The only calculation possible on these lines suggests that young medical doctors in Sri Lanka are paid the same in relation to the national average as are young doctors in the USA.

For international comparisons of health and education resources we make use of two sets of data, one from national income accounts, concerns public expenditure. It is very likely that in many countries, particularly where semi-government and especially, in the health field, social security systems are operating, this is understated. The greater centralisation of such expenditures in Sri Lanka may exaggerate their relative importance. The other set of data concerns household expenditures which certainly for health, but more rarely for education, exceed public expenditure.

Table 2: Public and private expenditure on education and health as a share of GDP, 1970 (per cent)

	Education			Health			Education and health		
	Public	Private	Total	Public	Private	Total	Public	Private	Total
Sudan	4.1	0.7	4.8	2.2	1.5	3.7	6.3	2.2	8.5
India	0.8	1.05	1.85	0.4	2.1	2.5	1.2	3.15	4.35
South Korea	0.2	4.2	4.4	0.05	2.0	2.05	0.25	6.2	6.45
Pakistan	0.9	0.9	1.8	0.9	1.5	2.4	1.8	2.4	4.2
Honduras	3.3	1.6	4.9	1.9	3.2	5.1	5.2	6.5	11.7
Sri Lanka	3.5	1.6	5.1	1.8	1.2	3.0	5.3	2.8	8.1
Philippines	2.4	2.4	4.8	0.4	1.5	1.9	2.8	3.9	6.7

Source: UN, Yearbook of National Accounts; ILO, Household Income and Expenditure Statistics

Taking first health, it appears that total resource inputs in Sri Lanka are by no means high. Sri Lanka ranks slightly higher than India but below the Sudan and Honduras. Indeed total health expenditures are fairly clustered around the 2-3 per cent of GNP level. Total expenditure on education in Sri Lanka is the highest of the 7 countries whose data are presented, but the differences between Sri Lanka (5.1 per cent) and Honduras (4.9 per cent) the Sudan (4.8 per cent) and the Philippines (4.8 per cent) are pretty minor. Nevertheless India and Pakistan, which, internationally, rate fairly well on total health expenditure, come very low on total education expenditure. However, it still does not appear that total resources devoted to health and education, while relatively high in Sri Lanka, are that far out of step.

But turning from a discussion of total resources to the origin of resources suggests that the role of the State has been unusually important in Sri Lanka. The commitment of public resources to health has accounted for around 60 per cent of total expenditure and of public resources to education some 70 per cent of the total. For health, the Sudan nearly reached this percentage of public to total expenditure but the others were far below. For education the Sudan exceeded this share of public expenditure in total expenditure while Honduras nearly reached it. Generally, one might say that governments have been far more willing to take a large burden of educational financing than of health financing.

The fact that government financing is a significant share of total financing does not guarantee, even in Sri Lanka, that health and education services are distributed independently of income. It has certainly been claimed in relation to e.g. government health expenditures in the Philippines that these are concentrated on high quality hospitals in major cities and have had few benefits for the bulk of the population.[1] Similarly where the total level of resources, public and private, still remains meagre and insufficient under any criterion it is unlikely that the services they provide will be equally available to all. Nevertheless for Sri Lanka the relatively high level of total resources for health and education and the relatively high share of government financing in these resources are no doubt crucial explanatory variables for the country's high aggregate welfare level.

---

[1] See E. Tan, "Taxation, Government Spending and Income Distribution in the Philippines", Geneva, ILO, 1975, World Employment Programme research working paper (restricted).

Just as large amounts of public resources have been devoted to
health and education programmes they have equally been used generously
to finance food consumption. The official "net food subsidy" has generally amounted to some 10 per cent of private food consumption. One
can ask how Governments have been able to finance such a programme.
Firstly, of course, the calories consumed in Sri Lanka are by no
means all produced there. Around 40 per cent are imported and, when
netted out with domestic procurement for the rice ration, sold at a loss.
Hence the concept of the net food subsidy arises. That domestic food production is relatively low is caused largely in its turn by the export
orientation of plantation agriculture and its generally higher level of
productivity. In the late 1950s plantation agriculture was estimated to
be five times as efficient as domestic agriculture in meeting food needs.[1]
The differential probably halved by the late 1960s[2] and is almost certainly
lower today. That so much food was imported in fact eased administrative
distributional problems and gave the State its opportunity to establish
a system of guaranteed rations.

Corresponding to the major role of foreign trade in the economy the
level of domestic resource mobilisation by the public sector was, and has
remained, high. Originally the bulk of current receipts was from export
and import taxes. In more recent years internal activities have borne a
higher share of the tax burden. However, the share of GNP taken as
government current receipts has changed little. It was some 24 per cent in
the mid-1950s, some 27 per cent in the mid-1960s and 23 per cent in the
mid-1970s. Thus, on every side Governments have had the opportunity to
undertake welfare programmes.

Some welfare indicators through time

The availability of resources to Governments of Sri Lanka at a high
level suggests that welfare levels have been high throughout a considerable
period. This can be followed up for the two programmes of health care
and education. For health considerable improvements in health states have
taken place over the last 50 years at least, as Table 3 demonstrates. It

---

[1] N. Kaldor, "Papers by visiting economists", Planning Secretariat,
Colombo 1959.

[2] P. Richards, Employment and unemployment in Ceylon, OECD, Paris
1971.

was, in fact, during the immediate post-war and early independence period
that age-specific death rates fell most quickly. This was more true even
for adults during that period than for children. The major cause of death
in 1945, infectious, parasitic and respiratory diseases, fell from an
incidence of 0.5 per cent to 0.2 per cent in 1955. Malarial deaths (incidence 0.13 per cent) almost disappeared. Pneumonia (incidence 0.14 per
cent) was halved as were infant convulsions (0.19 per cent). Mortality
rates have fallen further, but by no means so dramatically, since 1955.

Table 3: Age-specific death rates males, selected ages and periods

Age group	1920-22	1945-47	1952-54	1971
Under 1	226.9	147.1	96.8	54.0
1 - 4	46.7	24.9	17.1	5.1
20 - 24	10.4	5.5	2.2	2.2
40 - 44	20.5	11.8	4.8	5.4
60 - 64	47.5	34.2	21.5	21.3

Source: UN ESCAP, Population of Sri Lanka, Country Monograph Series, No. 4
Bangkok 1976.

The reasons for the decline in mortality from 1945-1952 have been
hotly debated. Malaria eradication had many indirect beneficial effects
since malaria-occasioned debilitation raised the likelihood of death from
other diseases. Nevertheless improvements in food supplies and a better
hospital and medical network are also credited with contributing independently
to the mortality decline.[1]

Turning now to age-specific school enrolment rates and rates of progression between grades the position is not quite so rosy. Table 4 shows
how school enrolment for the age-group 5-9 was hardly higher in 1974 than
in 1955. Conversely teenage enrolment was higher, significantly so for
the 15-19 age-group. This stagnation in primary school enrolment suggests
the presence of some fairly serious obstacles standing in the way of expansion of that level of education. This is confirmed by the data on progression rates. Of the 1971 entrants some 63 per cent were left (in 1975)

---

[1] These reasons are discussed comprehensively in the UN ESCAP monograph mentioned as the source of Table 3.

in grade V. If this implies five years of schooling and should therefore be
compared with grade IV enrolments in the 1950s then very little had changed
between those years. Nor, if we take retention to grade VIII, 34 per cent
for those entering in 1955 and 41 per cent for those entering in 1968 (not
shown in the table), had there been major improvements. In secondary education a major change occurred between 1952 (i.e. those reaching grade XII in
1956) and 1960 (i.e. those reaching grade XII in 1964). Since then the
situation has been fairly stable.

Table 4: Educational enrolment and progression rates

Enrolment rates	1952	1955	1959	1966	1971	1974
Age 5- 9	n.a.	72.2	77.9	n.a.	84.5	73.3
Age 10-14	n.a.	54.5	60.5	n.a.	71.2	65.1
Age 15-19	n.a.	11.5	14.7	n.a.	16.3	22.2
Progression rates[1]						
Grade IA	100	100	100	-	-	-
Grade IB	73	75	75	100	100	-
Grade IV	52	59	58	70	76	-
Grade V	45	52	53	69	63	-
Grade VIII	30	34	33	47	-	-

Grade VIII	100	100	100	100	100	-
Grade XII	5	9	15	16	21	-

Source: UN ESCAP, op. cit.

[1] i.e. of 100 pupils enrolled in grade I in 1952, 30 per cent
finally reached grade VIII

District level indicators

Table 5 allows a geographical overview of certain welfare indicators
on a district level. The table gives certain background variables for each
district, i.e. population density, per cent of population resident in urban
areas and the share of population resident on estates. Many of these might
be compared to large villages, but with fewer facilities. In particular, at
this time estates were running their own schools, which never went above grade
VI. The table gives two educational indicators, retention in grade VI over
grade II and repetition in grade I. If requirements for passing from grade I
to grade II are standard throughout the island (which they almost certainly
were not) this gives some indication of the "success" of grade I education.
The data on chronic undernutrition are from a survey of 13,450 pre-school
children. In addition we give the Registrar General's statistics on infant

mortality and on female life expectancy. The presence of a sizeable estate population in any district has a significant effect on the level of all of these health indicators.

One can begin with the four districts running south from Colombo to Matara, very densely populated and highly urbanised with a minor estate population. They were generally successful in retaining children in school and avoiding repetition in grade I. Infant mortality was low and female life expectancy high. Chronic undernutrition was below the national level. Such districts will inevitably score higher than average. The next group of districts in Table 1, from Ratnapura to Matale, are in from the coast and contain the bulk of the estate population, which reaches its peak in Nuwara Eliya. They are fairly densely populated but not highly urbanised. In government, i.e. non-estate, schools retention remains fairly high although repetition is variable. Infant mortality is everywhere above average (and female life expectancy virtually everywhere below average). Furthermore infant mortality would appear to have fallen over the twenty year period (early 1950s to early 1970s) considerably less than elsewhere. These health indicators are conspicuously unfavourable in Nuwara Eliya. Chronic under-nutrition is often very high.

The next two, west coast, districts Kurunegala and Puttalam are different again. Not very densely populated nor urbanised, they are relatively successful educationally and have low infant mortality and high female life expectancy rates. The next three, the main Tamil speaking districts, Mannar to Jaffna, are relatively similar despite their varying population densities. Educational retention is low in Mannar and Vavuniya, and not very high in Jaffna, but infant mortality is everywhere low and has fallen dramatically. Batticaloa and Trincomalee, the two major east coast districts, both, in fact, highly urbanised, are educationally extremely unsuccessful. Batticaloa, in addition, has the highest infant mortality and chronic undernutrition rate outside the estate areas. The next three districts, Pollonaruwa, Anuradhapura and Amparai, are the areas of major new resettlement and irrigation schemes. While not successful in educational terms they have achieved low mortality levels. The last two, central-southern districts, Moneregala and Hambantota have low infant mortality and a mixed educational record.

Perhaps two major features stand out in this description. One is the correlation of a high share of estate population with high levels of infant mortality. The other is that educational retention in government schools seems to fall with increasing distance from Colombo.

Table 5 : Selected district-level indicators, early 1970s

	Pop. density[1]	Per cent urban[2]	Estate pop.[3]	Grade VI/II[4]	Repet. grade I[5]	Chronic under-nutrition[6]	Inf. mort.[7] 1952-54	Inf. mort.[7] 1970-74	Female life exp.[8]
Colombo	3,270	55	1	75	20	21	71	42	68
Kalutara	1,169	22	7	62	22	27	56	41	71
Galle	1,128	21	4	66	23	33	68	46	71
Matara	1,214	11	4	66	27	30	54	38	71
Ratnapura	520	8	22	56	28	37	72	63	63
Kegalle	1,019	7	13	68	25	40	71	51	69
Kandy	1,265	12	30	63	27	50	87	67	62
Nuwara Eliya	911	6	60	67	30	n.a.	106	92	55
Badulla	544	9	39	65	35	49	81	61	62
Matale	406	12	17	49	34	39	84	55	64
Kurunegala	556	4	2	61	24	30	70	40	69
Puttalam	323	14	2	50	30	24	59	36	68
Mannar	77	14	-	40	37	n.a.	100	41	63
Vavuniya	63	22	-	40	36	30	73	28	66
Jaffna	700	33	-	55	30	28	67	26	67
Batticaloa	253	27	-	32	41	36	97	52	60
Trincomalee	181	38	-	38	44	n.a.	78	37	65
Pollonaruwa	123	10	-	40	29	n.a.	74	29	69
Anuradhapura	138	10	-	46	50	31	74	38	69
Amparai	230	12	3	48	24	n.a.	97	39	67
Moneregala	68	3	9	40	32	n.a.	81	35	69
Hambantota	337	10	-	55	29	n.a.	58	35	69
All-Island	509	22.4	10.8	50	27	35	74	47	67

Source: Department of Census and Statistics, Census of Population 1963 and 1971; Statistical Abstract of Ceylon, 1970-1971; Bulletin on Vital Statistics 1976; Ministry of Education, Medium Term Plan for Education, Colombo 1973; UN ESCAP, op. cit.

[1] Population density 1970; persons per square mile.

[2] Urbanisation rate 1971, per cent.

[3] Population resident on estates 1963, per cent.

[4] Numbers in grade VI as compared to grade II, 1971 (government schools only).

[5] Repetition in grade I, 1971 (government schools only), per cent.

[6] Chronic undernutrition in pre-school children from the Sri Lanka nutrition status survey, 1975-1976, prepared by the US Department of Health, Education and Welfare in co-operation with the Government of Sri Lanka, CARE and USAID.

[7] Infant mortality, per mille, average of years given.

[8] Female life expectancy at birth, in years.

This basic needs geographical tour of Sri Lanka serves further to remind us of one thing. The rest of the analysis in this chapter will be undertaken in terms of income groups and of the three statistically recognised sectors, urban, rural and estate. These three areas go far to capture the major characteristics of different modes of living and of the organisation of working relationships. Yet, particularly in the rural sector, there is clearly some difference between a village in Colombo district and one in Batticaloa. It is likely, for example, that the over-all stagnation in educational enrolment that has already been observed, is partly caused by a different appreciation of the role of education in less populated areas.

Welfare and income levels

(i) Food consumption

Sri Lanka has never undertaken a nationwide survey specifically of food consumption. Small-scale nutrition enquiries have been held but for nation-wide comparable information use must be made of either the Socio-economic Survey of 1969-70 or the Consumer Finance Survey of 1973. Neither survey could carry out the very meticulous work of checking current food consumption meal by meal. However, it would appear that in the Consumer Finance Survey visits were made three times to households during the reference week. In the Socio-economic Survey "daily records were kept". However, in fact the Socio-economic Survey, which is in many ways more likely to be accurate than the Consumer Finance Survey,[1] recorded generally higher consumption levels for all foodstuffs (except wheat flour). While it is certainly possible that for some items consumption had fallen between the two survey periods, it is highly unlikely that it had fallen across the board, including consumption of chillies, vegetables, coconuts, tea, milk, meat, onions and fish. Given that there is a general presumption of under-estimation from both surveys, compared to data on availability of food-stuffs, it seems preferable to rely generally on the Socio-economic Survey's results.

Nevertheless, as has already been mentioned, over-all food availability depends considerably on imports. As a result fluctuations in consumption of rice, flour, bread and, perhaps most of all, of sugar, can be expected. Given that there have been many twists and turns in the government food distribution programmes, it seems preferable, not necessarily to insist on the use of the most up-to-date information regardless of its reliability, but to examine in detail the effects of the system as it was operating in 1969/70

---

[1] In addition the Consumer Finance Survey covered only 3 months of the year while the 1969/70 Socio-economic Survey was undertaken in four quarterly rounds.

when 2 lbs of rice per week were given to everyone aged over one year.

A first step is to compare average per capita daily calories from the Socio-economic Survey (SES) with those of the Food Balance Sheet (FBS) published in the Statistical Abstract of Ceylon for the same year. The data taken are an average for 1969 and 1970. There are discrepancies between the two sources which suggest that the use of food balance sheets may give unreliable information on consumption trends. While the over-all calorie level is very similar, it is likely that the FBS may exaggerate final consumption, possibly because of inadequate knowledge of stocks or wastage. Furthermore, the FBS may ignore some individually small items in the "other" category. Opinion differs on the necessary daily average calorie intake for Sri Lanka. Some authorities give 2,100 calories and 45 grams of protein, some 2,200 and 48 grams. We have taken a figure of 2,169 calories, although we recognise that requirements vary considerably in line with energy used up and different climatic conditions.[1]

Table 6: Calories per caput per day, 1969/70

	SES	per cent	FBS	per cent
Cereals	1,221	53.9	1,348	59.4
Oil and oil-bearing nuts	502	22.2	386	17.0
Pulses	52	2.3	59	2.6
Sugar	200	8.8	238	10.5
Yams/potatoes	30	1.3	73	3.2
Other	259	11.5	164	7.3
	2,264	100.0	2,268	100.0

Source: FAO, Income and Food Consumption, Report to the Government of Sri Lanka, 1973, and Statistical Abstract of Ceylon, 1970-71.

Before proceeding further it is necessary to standardise family composition. While the SES data are presented on a per capita basis the demographic characteristics of an "average person" may be expected to vary between income groups and sectors. After dividing the population into two sex groups and six age groups, weights were applied. The weights were in fact taken from other (Philippines) recommendations on calorie requirements, since data for Sri Lanka were not available.[2] The composition of different income groups in terms of their demographic/calorie requirements is given in Table 7.

---

[1] This figure was reached using age-specific targets given by the Food and Nutrition Institute, Manila (1976) weighted by the age distribution of Sri Lanka's population.

[2] Ibid.

The data in Table 7 are standardised by sector. In fact sectoral averages are almost identical. The data show that the average person in a poor household generally belonged to an age-sex group which is generally accepted as requiring fewer calories. The converse usually applies to richer households. As a result the data on the distribution of per capita calorie intake presented later have been standardised to assume the same age-sex breakdown in each income group.

Table 7: Weighted demographic composition per caput

Urban		Rural		Estate	
Income group[1]	Coef-ficient	Income group	Coef-ficient	Income group	Coef-ficient
1.8	0.98	6.2	1.01	5.7	0.97
4.9	0.97	14.6	0.97	21.3	0.98
9.2	0.96	17.0	0.99	24.4	0.98
39.7	0.99	39.9	1.00	41.5	1.02
19.7	1.02	14.6	1.04	6.0	1.03
9.5	1.03	4.9	1.03	(	
5.7	1.02	(2.8	1.02	(1.1	1.07
9.4	1.03	(		(	
100.0	1.00	100.0	1.00	100.0	1.00

Source: See text.

[1] Here, and in the following tables, the income groups are the share of population in the various original household income groups, e.g. Rs 0-99, 100-150, etc. Since the same absolute income limits were used for each sector the share of population in the various income groups varies considerably. Thus in estate areas 5.7 per cent of population fell in the group Rs 0-99 compared to only 1.8 per cent in urban areas.

Table 8 shows the distribution by income group of both total calories and total protein. These data on distribution by income group are presented before data on absolute levels largely because they can be considered more reliable. It must be stressed, as will be apparent below, that the distribution data are given sector by sector. Subject to that proviso the data show a fairly equal distribution pattern. However, the poorest urban 7 per cent and rural 21 per cent still receive significantly below their proportionate share especially for proteins. The relatively equal distribution within each sector must be put down to a number of factors including obviously the supply of free rice but also homogeneity in dietary habits.

That protein distribution is also fairly equal is perhaps less expected. However, this is due partly to the large share (some 60 per cent) of proteins from cereals, the relatively equal distribution of coconut consumption and a consumption of dried fish (supplying around 10 per cent of protein) biassed if anything towards the poor. Conversely, meat, the more obviously income elastic source of protein, gives only a negligible quantity of protein.

Table 8: Calorie and protein distribution (per cent)

Urban			Rural			Estate		
Income group	Calories	Proteins	Income group	Calories	Proteins	Income group	Calories	Proteins
1.8	1.4	1.4	6.2	5.0	4.8	5.7	5.6	5.3
4.9	4.4	4.1	14.6	14.1	13.9	21.3	21.1	20.1
9.2	8.8	8.8	17.0	16.2	16.2	24.4	23.8	23.4
39.7	38.5	37.9	39.9	40.7	40.8	41.5	41.9	43.6
19.7	20.0	20.0	14.6	15.2	15.3	6.0	6.2	6.0
9.5	10.0	9.9	4.9	5.4	5.5	(		
5.7	6.4	6.5	(			(1.1	1.4	1.5
9.4	10.6	11.3	(2.8	3.3	3.4	(		
100.0	100.1	100.0	100.0	99.9	99.9	100.0	100.0	99.9

Source: Socio-economic Survey, 1969-70

Table 9 presents data on actual and desired calorie intake by income group. The column of desired intake represents the average desired quantity, 2,169, standardised for income group by using the coefficients of Table 7.

It must be noted in relation to Table 9, that "desired" calories are not calculated in relation to the varying energy expenditure of different occupations and tasks. This caveat is particularly applicable to estates.

The first response to Table 9 is that there would appear to be an obvious calorie deficiency for the poorest four urban income groups - some 56 per cent of the urban population. Probably around 10 per cent of the urban population has a very serious over-all calorie deficiency. In rural areas the break-even point is reached more quickly but the same remarks probably apply to the poorest 10 per cent. The picture in estate areas is very different.

However, over-all the message from Table 9 is that in comparison with rural average, the urban sector is considerably undernourished - probably right up to a part of the income group third from the top. However, in comparison with estate areas the rural sector is undernourished, again right up to a part of the fourth income group from the top. These observations cast some doubt on the over-all adequacy of a target figure of 2,169 calories. It is also possible that particularly urban consumption is seriously underestimated. More specifically the estate daily intake is from 300-400 calories higher than the rural intake, partly, on the supply side, because estate workers purchase wheat flour from estate shops, and on the demand side, because of the full-time work put in by both men and women. This last point is important. Estate workers need to work hard, but so do rural workers in general. At a guess, which unfortunately cannot be confirmed, female workers on estates consume very considerably more food than female workers elsewhere. Perhaps this is one explanation of e.g. the traditionally small share of rice transplanted, because most rural women have not been strong enough to do the work.

Table 9 : **Actual and desired calorie intake**

Urban			Rural			Estate		
Income group	Actual	Desired	Income group	Actual	Desired	Income group	Actual	Desired
1.8	1,632	2,099	6.2	1,881	2,189	5.7	2,285	2,089
4.9	1,870	2,091	14.6	2,137	2,117	21.3	2,271	2,116
9.2	1,972	2,073	17.0	2,146	2,151	24.4	2,241	2,123
39.7	2,067	2,129	39.9	2,326	2,180	41.5	2,411	2,199
19.7	2,230	2,183	14.6	2,467	2,263	6.0	2,471	2,223
9.5	2,340	2,205	4.9	2,598	2,245	(		
5.7	2,451	2,202	(			(1.1	3,220	2,313
9.4	2,496	2,217	(2.8	2,735	2,216	(		
100.0	2,162	2,169	100.0	2,268	2,169	100.0	2,426	2,169

Source: See text.

One must conclude that while the distribution of calorie intake is not so very skewed, and income perhaps plays less part in allocating calorie consumption than it might,[1] nevertheless a desired pattern of calorie intake

---

[1] One can compare some data from India. Ranking households in terms of total consumption expenditure the poorest 20 per cent consumed only 12 per cent of total calories and the richest 20 per cent consumed some 30 per cent. The data are for 1958 and are given in Poverty and Income Distribution in India, ed. T.N. Srinivasan and P.K. Bardhan, Calcutta, 1974.

would require a distribution benefitting much more the poorer groups, especially, one suspects, the rural poor.

Turning to the adequacy of protein intake, Table 10 gives data on actual protein intake, estimated from the SES.

Table 10: Actual protein intake in grams

Urban		Rural		Estate	
Income group	Protein	Income group	Protein	Income group	Protein
1.8	37.2	6.2	40.3	5.7	52.2
4.9	41.0	14.6	47.3	21.3	53.9
9.2	45.8	17.0	48.6	24.4	54.7
39.7	47.7	39.9	52.5	41.5	62.3
19.7	51.9	14.6	56.0	6.0	59.9
9.5	54.8	4.9	59.0	(	
5.7	59.1	(		(1.1	83.2
9.4	62.6	(2.8	63.7	(	
100.0	52.2	100.0	51.2	100.0	61.6

Source: See text.

The recommended figure for protein intake is 45-48 grams. On this measure it is only the very poorest who are deficient in protein. The higher figures for protein consumption on the estates are in large part due to their higher cereal consumption. However, the poor on estates also consume nearly twice as many pulses as the rural poor in general. However, while the poor on estates may be consuming the desirable level of protein some 75 per cent of their protein comes from cereals so that their diet is hardly balanced. The same point can of course be made for the dietary pattern in Sri Lanka over-all; to have 70 per cent of protein from cereals is widespread among rich and poor alike.

There is no need to look in much further detail at food intake. It can certainly, however, be noted that the recommended target for meat, 0.7 lbs. per month, was met only by the top 5 per cent approximately in rural areas, and 10 per cent on estates although in urban areas only the poorest 40 per cent did not reach it.[1] The target for pulses was apparently met nowhere. It is, on the other hand, ironic that every single income group surpassed

---

[1] Information not given in tables.

the target for sugar, some 2 lbs. per month; ironic because the great bulk of sugar is imported. However, sugar consumption may well have fallen considerably during the 1970s.

Certainly the Sri Lanka Department of Nutrition considers the diet of around half of the population of the country inadequate. Various surveys have pointed to high rates of nutritional anaemia in pregnant women and to the high frequency of low birth weight babies among the poor. The Department of Nutrition considers average per capita calorie intake sufficient. Obviously, as noted, the distribution of calorie intake means that many people fall below the average.

(ii) Education

The aim of this section is to discuss the importance of household income in determining access to the education system. To make full use of State provided educational services requires a mix of incentives which the State alone cannot provide. Facilities must be close and reasonably attractive, the differential benefits in-school arising from home background variables must be minimised and parents must be convinced that education will have benefits beyond a "baby-sitting" function which will improve their children's chances in future life. In this respect parental occupation and, what is closely related, parental education level, will influence the views of parents and children on the value of education. It is therefore extremely unlikely that home income effects will ever disappear as a determinant of access to education.

Ideally the role of education would be discussed not in terms of who attends school but of the contribution of schooling to the development of a child's abilities. This would require information on ability test scores at different ages. The only approximation available to data of that nature is retention in the higher reaches of the education system where ability plays a role in continued presence at school. But the "open access" span still covers the first nine years of education. In this section the income variable used, and which will be used in the rest of this Chapter, relates to quintiles of population, ranked by ascending per capita income.

The first data we present, in Table 11, show enrolment rates of two different age-groups, by income level, and the ratio between them. In this table the section "rural" also includes "estate", thus allowing better international comparisons. For the first age-group, 6-14, enrolment rates

are universally fairly high but tend to rise with income, most in estate
areas, least in urban areas. For rural and estate areas rates for girls
are below those for boys in all income groups. For urban areas the difference is still there but is only very slight. For the second age-group,
15-17, the differences become far more marked. Urban males have the highest
enrolment rates of all and income plays a more important role. Income,
however, probably plays a more important part in influencing the enrolment
of rural males. Income also comes to play a major part in determining the
enrolment of girls, particularly in rural areas. In estate areas very few
girls of this age-group are in school. As a result of these features the
ratio between the two enrolment rates is highest in urban areas, for males,
and rises significantly with income level.

For ease of exposition Table 11 uses two age-group averages. Studying
the data by single years shows children of the very poorest group, i.e. the
bottom quintile, tend to enter school late. Their enrolment rate peaks at
age 9 or 10 with some 85 per cent enrolment. For the richest quintile
enrolment peaks at age 8 with 95 per cent enrolment. The effect of income
appears strongest in the transition between ages 10 and 16. In the richest
quintile some two-thirds of the 10 year old group are still at school at
age 16. For the poorest group only 40 per cent remains. Nevertheless it
remains true that some five per cent of the children of the rich never
attend school and that at age 14, some 30 per cent of them are out of
school. Conversely at age 18 nearly 25 per cent of the children of the
poorest group are still at school.

An investigation of the reasons for non-attendance was made in an
official survey of 1959.[1] Its report came to few concrete conclusions
beyond stating that "contrary to popular belief, lack of schools is not one
of the major problems of non-attendance". In the recommendations of the
report stress is laid on greater compulsion in school attendance and the need
for more imaginative curricula. In a questionnaire given to parents of
5,140 children of school age not attending school there was a choice of
34 responses. Taking only the primary response these can be categorised

---

[1] Report of the Committee on Non-School-Going Children, S.P. III,
Colombo 1960.

Table 11: Enrolment and retention rates: rural, estate and urban areas, 1969/70 (percentage)

| Quintile group | Rural[1] | | | | | | Estate | | | | | | Urban | | | | | |
| | Males | | | Females | | | Males | | | Females | | | Males | | | Females | | |
	I	II	II/I	I	II	II/I	I	II	II/I	I	II	II/I	I	II	II/I	I	II	II/I
0 - 20	80	43	54	71	32	45	59	21	36	47	9	19	83	56	67	85	42	50
20 - 40	84	44	53	79	38	47	73	26	36	57	7	12	88	57	65	83	45	54
40 - 60	87	55	63	81	44	54	76	33	43	63	14	22	92	59	65	88	49	55
60 - 80	85	55	65	82	50	61	73	25	-	59	11	18	93	71	76	87	50	57
80 - 100	90	61	68	85	59	70	76	8	-	63	22	35	87	71	82	87	62	72

Source: Department of Census and Statistics, op. cit.

I = age group 6 - 14
II = age group 15 - 17

[1] Including estate.

[2] Here, and in all tables using quintile group data, the limits to the quintiles are given by the national, all-island income distribution. Thus the urban sector will be consistently over-weighted in the higher quintile groups and the other sectors in the poorer quintile groups.

as follows:

    i) Poverty: 40 per cent. (Includes "parents cannot affort to maintain children in school", "cannot afford to buy books", etc.)

    ii) Relative priorities: 31 per cent. (These factors may be the corollary of poverty, but not necessarily, i.e. "parents find continued education not worthwhile", "wish the children to help them at home", "home circumstances are so difficult".)

    iii) Unsuitable curriculum: 9 per cent. (This includes "pupils do not consider education worthwhile".)

    iv) Illness and physical handicaps: 7 per cent.

    v) Physical access: 4 per cent. (Includes no schools within two miles, no transport, no roads in remote areas.)

    vi) Other: 9 per cent.

As one might anticipate poverty emerges as the most important single factor, but given the extent of non-attendance among the rich, it probably does not, in this context, explain even a majority of the non-attendance.

As has already been hinted the advantage of the rich may come not only from greater staying power within the education system, which is clearly there, but also from a relatively more successful performance within it. This can only be inferred from the data in Table 12. This shows, for children in school, their rate of progression through the system, which is partly because of age differences and partly because of ability differences. Thus at age 14 only 4 per cent of children from richer households were still in primary grades, compared to 26 per cent of children from the poorest households. Similarly at age 18, over 40 per cent from the richest group had passed "O" level, compared to 10 per cent from the poorest.

Table 12: Age and grade of education, children in school, 1969/71 (per cent)

Age/grade completed	Income group		
	Poorest quintile	Medium quintile	Richest quintile
12 Primary	57	44	29
Middle	44	56	71
14 Primary	26	22	4
Middle	73	78	93
"O" level	1	-	3
16 Primary	16	6	3
Middle	81	87	86
"O" level	2	6	10
18 Primary	8	-	1
Middle	82	74	57
"O" level	10	26	39
"A" level	-	-	3

Source: Department of Census and Statistics, op. cit.

There are very many things which can be said about education in Sri Lanka but we shall keep a discussion of education policies until a later chapter. Meanwhile, we can present data showing how the composition of university admission changed during the 1950s and 1960s. This analysis, however, can only be made in terms of population groups and not income groups.

We have already noted that Sri Lanka is a multi-ethnic country with the predominant population group Sinhalese, who are nearly all either Buddhist or Christian, followed by Ceylon and Indian Tamils, either Hindu or Christian, with smaller groups of Muslims and Burghers (generally Christian). "Christian" is likely, but by no means necessarily, to be closely associated with urban areas and with low-country wet zone areas, and more loosely associated with higher than average income groups. Among the richer groups "Christian" was associated with knowledge, and use, of the English language. Table 13 shows the breakdown of the total population by these groups in the early 1950s and late 1960s and university admission in 1950 and 1967.

Table 13: **Population and university admission, Sri Lanka, per cent**

Population group	Share of population		Share of admission	
	c1950	c1967	1950	1967
Sinhalese Buddhists	64.3	66.3	48.6	79.2
Sinhalese Christians	5.2	4.7	18.0	4.9
Ceylon Tamil Hindus	7.5	7.8	15.6	10.8
Ceylon Tamil Christians	3.4	3.3	8.9	3.3
Indian Tamils[1]	12.4	10.6	1.4	0.1
Muslims	6.0	6.7	1.9	1.4
Burghers[2]	1.2	0.6	5.6	0.3
Total	100.0	100.0	100.0	100.0

Source: Uswatte Arachchi: Modern Asian Studies, July 1974.

[1] Assuming no Indian Tamils are Christian.

[2] Including other.

In the early 1950s when most secondary and all university education was in English the various Christian groups, as well as Ceylon Tamil Hindus, were proportionately over-represented in university admission. Sinhalese Buddhists were significantly under-represented as were Indian Tamils, and to a lesser extent, Muslims. These last two groups continued to be considerably under-represented into the late 1960s. Education facilities for Indian Tamils failed to improve while many Muslims held an ambivalent attitude towards university education.

Almost certainly the main change during the period 1950-1967 was the extension of instruction in Sinhalese to nearly all secondary schools and to the university. Language streaming still permitted instruction in Tamil and in English for Burghers, a few others, and those Muslims who chose it. By 1967 university admissions for Christian groups reflected very closely their population shares. Sinhalese Buddhists obviously made great strides and by 1967 were over-represented.

(iii) Health standards and health care

Unfortunately this section will hardly be able to live up to the promise of its title. The Socio-economic Survey is the only source of data disaggregated by income level which at all reflects these issues. Even so the information it primarily sought was on "illness", which may not reflect well the severity of different health states. On health care the survey distinguished types of treatment by ayurvedic and western (thereby omitting some faith healing treatments) and government and private. But it does not, for example, distinguish between physician visits, nurse consultations or even pharmacists' recommendations. Information of this sort, which would be necessary to examine in detail how the various income groups benefit from existing health services, would need a specialist survey. In this survey the basic question asked was how many household members had suffered any illness in the past two weeks. From this question the results are as follows:

Table 14: Incidence of illness by quintile of income per capita (per cent)

Quintile	Urban	Rural	Estate	Total
I	4.9	8.6	7.8	8.2
II	3.6	6.9	7.0	6.5
III	5.7	7.9	3.7	7.0
IV	7.1	7.4	5.8	7.2
V	5.9	9.5	5.9	8.2
Av.	5.7	8.0	6.0	7.4

Source: Department of Census and Statistics, Socio-economic Survey, op. cit.

As will be evident from much of this discussion, inter-sectoral differences are very important here. Among the poorest two income groups incidence was least in urban areas, on average, however, urban areas and estate areas record similar figures. Among the rich the rural sector leads. Within each sector there is very little evidence of any connection between income and illness. The rural sector clearly, and the two poorest estate income groups, are most illness prone. This would not seem to correlate well with what we know of their food intake, when, after all, urban areas seemed to consume least, but it probably does tie in with the subject of the next section, drinking water and sanitary facilities. Again it does not seem to tie in with the data on infant mortality given in Table 1 where non-estate rural areas show up well. The greater incidence of illness in rural

areas and among the poorer estate groups was slightly associated with
fewer long absences from normal duties, as Table 15 shows.

Table 15 : Absence from normal duties caused by illness , by quintile

	Urban			Rural			Estate		
	- 1 wk	1-4 wks	1 mth +	- 1 wk	1-4 wks	1 mth +	- 1 wk	1-4 wks	1 mth +
I	57	29	14	61	34	5	60	34	6
II	58	40	2	63	32	5	55	39	6
III	53	40	7	59	36	5	53	40	7
IV	63	29	8	59	35	6	51	39	10
V	56	34	10	61	35	4	54	39	7

Source: As Table 14 .

However, it is unlikely that this was sufficient to compensate for the
higher level of disease incidence and thus reduce the over-all higher cost
of illness per person in rural areas.

As noted, the information to be given in Table 16 on source of health care
is conceptually deficient. It is possible that although only 54 per cent
of total contacts for the whole country (a figure not given in the table)
were with the government sector, a greater share of physician contacts
were with the public sector. However, it is also extremely likely that
many "non-western" sources of health care treatment were not faithfully
reported.[1] However, the share of contacts with government provided medicine
varied little with income group although they were somewhat higher in rural
areas.   Of course, the question of preferred source of
treatment can hardly be separated from that of available source of treatment. Thus the high share of "private western" in estate areas is probably
caused by the absence of government facilities and the same applies to
"private ayurvedic" in rural areas. Total "ayurvedic" it can be noted
accounts for as much as 16 per cent of contacts for the richest urban group
(and 26 per cent for the poorest rural group).

---

[1] See Agrarian Research and Training Institute, "A study of four
villages", R.D. Wanigaratne, Colombo 1978. This report found that 18 per
cent of sampled villagers used only faith healing treatment.

Table 16: Source of health care

	Urban			Rural			Estate		
	I[1]	III	V	I	III	V	I	III	V
Government:									
Ayurvedic	5	7	6	5	6	6	2	2	2
Western	45	42	40	50	53	51	48	40	46
Total	50	49	46	55	58	57	50	42	48
Private:									
Ayurvedic	12	13	10	21	18	14	4	3	4
Western	35	31	40	17	20	25	43	49	42
Total	48	45	50	38	38	39	46	53	46
Unspec.	2	6	4	6	4	4	3	5	6
Total	100	100	100	100	100	100	100	100	100

Source: As Table 14.

[1] Data are given for the poorest, middle and richest income groups

Home facilities and income levels

Tables 17, 18 and 19 on housing, toilet facilities and water, spell
out a few "home truths" about domestic facilities by quintile income group
of households. While data of this kind can be used to set programme targets
for public health measures over-all, they are a reminder of some of the
consequences of a low per capita output of goods and services and unequally
distributed purchasing power. Use of certain items reflects a partnership
between households and government in providing piped water or sewage systems.
The provision of such items then reflects government programme priorities and
the contrast between the relatively equal use of, say, primary education
facilities between income groups, and the use of toilet or bathing water
facilities in indicative.

Table 17 gives the number of persons per room for each sector by
quintile income group. Rural areas have the least congested housing and
one can assume that the rural data reflect by and large the influence of
income alone, i.e. there are few other space or administrative constraints.
In comparison, the urban poor are severely under-housed, while on estates
the scope for household control over housing space is minimal. For the
bulk of the population these data relate, of course, to conditions of ownership or tenancy. In urban areas some 45 per cent of the poorest household
income groups (up to Rs. 200) live in rented accommodation. In rural areas

the percentage, 4.5, is exactly one tenth of that. On estates, of course, accommodation is rent free. Thus, for the poor, in both urban and estate areas congested housing arises at least partly because of the absence of home-ownership.

Table 17: Persons per room by quintile of per capita income

	I	II	III	IV	V	Average
Urban	3.5	3.1	2.7	2.1	1.2	1.8
Rural	2.7	2.3	2.1	1.6	1.2	1.8
Estate	3.8	3.4	2.7	2.1	1.4	2.5

Source: As Table 14.

The toilet facility data are interesting as a guide to public health programmes (Table 18). Of course, the hygienic cost of "none" must vary between areas but it is certainly surprising that in urban areas and on estates this condition continues. The data demonstrate the urban bias in the construction of sewage systems for flush toilets. On estates one assumes that limited systems were installed by the owners.

Table 18: Toilet facilities by quintile of per capita income

	Urban			Rural			Estate		
	I	III	V	I	III	V	I	III	V
Flush	11	16	31	-	1	3	2	3	11
Bucket	29	29	25	1	2	4	4	5	5
Water seal or pit	35	38	38	49	58	72	64	65	71
None	25	19	6	50	39	21	30	27	13

Source: As Table 14.

The data on drinking water show that as much as 10 per cent of the urban poorest quintile have piped drinking water at home (Table 19). On estates the percentage is double. Yet on estates 12 per cent of the poorest group take drinking water from what is likely to be the most polluted source (although this need not be the case in the hills). In rural areas wells obviously predominate as a source of drinking water, although as many as 13 per cent of the poorest group do not even have access to well water. On estates "piped water" may be directly piped from a river or well, without any chemical treatment. In urban areas "piped water" implies treated water. These data do not therefore, tell much about the hygienic adequacy of the drinking water source. Turning to the source of water for personal bathing the main point is the much greater use of tanks or streams. Thus, as has already been suggested, while a source of water may be conveniently available in sufficient quantity for drinking, it may not be similarly available in sufficient quantity for bathing. This would seem to be particularly true on estates and for the poorest rural group.

Table 19: Source of water by quintile of per capita income

| | Drinking | | | | | | | | | Bathing | | | | | | | | |
| | Urban | | | Rural | | | Estate | | | Urban | | | Rural | | | Estate | | |
	I	III	V	I	III	V	I	III	V	I	III	V	I	III	V	I	III	V
Pipes inside	10	13	38	1	1	3	21	30	42	7	10	36	-	-	2	7	10	25
Pipes outside	43	41	25	4	3	2	50	45	36	28	25	16	1	1	1	2	4	5
Well	47	46	37	82	90	92	17	18	18	48	56	44	50	66	73	11	13	13
Tank or stream	-	-	-	13	6	3	12	7	3	17	9	4	49	33	24	80	73	57

Source: As Table 14.

Conclusion

The information given in the preceding section on home facilities shows the distribution of levels of basic needs satisfaction in the absence of major government programmes. It thus serves as a clear contrast to much of the information presented on the use of the major programmes of health care and education. Furthermore the income determined distribution of water or sanitary facilities is likely to raise the incidence of illness (even for a whole sector) and increase the burden on the health care programme. These facilities would seem to warrant more concentrated government effort.

However, the success of government intervention in food programmes, primary education and medical care must be acknowledged. Problems naturally remain particularly in secondary education where home background variables are very likely to affect educational outcomes. Furthermore handing out free food will by no means guarantee that that food is used to supplement and not to substitute for private food purchases. Nevertheless the major problem spotlighted in this chapter must remain the level of infant mortality and female life expectancy in estate areas.

PART II: Income Distribution and Poverty
CHAPTER 3
Income Distribution

A Revised Income Distribution for Sri Lanka

The objective of this chapter is to lay bare some of the major features
of income distribution in Sri Lanka. While we are only tangentially interested in how the degree of income inequality in Sri Lanka relates to other
countries, there are strong reasons for it, internationally speaking, to be
relatively low. Until 1975 a large part of the country's most valuable
assets were owned outside the country. As a result their net income did not
enter the accounts of resident households. After 1975 these assets passed
into State ownership so that, again, profits on them were outside the household sector and compensation for nationalisation was paid to non-resident
households. However, we shall firstly concentrate here on getting a little
closer to an accurate picture of the distribution of incomes before tax, not
including subsidised food (and government services) as income and taking the
consumption of home produced goods and services into account. Later parts
of the chapter will look at monetary and non-monetary income, at price shifts
and at food subsidies.

We shall work from the basic data provided by the Department of Census
and Statistics from the Socio-economic Survey undertaken in 1969/70. The
data are old but experience of other countries[1] strongly suggests that income
distributions do not change fast. The 1969/70 survey data also have advantages because firstly the original data tape is easy to utilise and secondly
that survey captured a higher share of total income (or at least of GDP at
factor cost), some 67 per cent, than did the 1973 Central Bank Consumer Finance
Survey, which captured some 61 per cent. In addition the 1969/70 survey recorded as consumption an amount equal to 91 per cent of private consumption in
the national income accounts. Invidious comparisons between surveys are not
in order here. The Consumer Finance Surveys very efficiently reconcile income
and expenditure totals but the Socio-economic Survey records greater consumption totals. More importantly, using this approach, between the two Consumer
Finance Surveys of 1963 and 1973 income coverage dropped from 67.5 per cent
to 61 per cent and consumption coverage from 86 per cent to 76 per cent. Any
analysis of intertemporal shifts based on data incorporating this decline
in over-all coverage is doomed to be unreliable.

Be this as it may any survey as usually published contains two major
sources of illusion. The first is the almost universal practice of ranking

---

[1] See, "The political economy of egalitarian growth", I. Adelman et al.,
Geneva, 1976.

households within the income distribution in terms of their total
income irrespective of whether they have one member or eleven. Hardly
ever are households ranked in terms of their per capita income.[1] But
since richer households are often larger households and poorer households smaller households, this means of statistical presentation exaggerates
the amount of "real" inequality. The second source of illusion is precisely
the degree of understatement of incomes. This can be measured roughly in
the aggregate, it can be estimated, using an input-output table, by income
source. But if there is any tendency for the poor to understate their
incomes (leaving aside their source of income) less than the rich, that bias
cannot be measured.

There is a third source of illusion in this particular survey which is
created by inclusion of servants as family members in the statistics, thus
lowering the per capita incomes of richer households. Allowance can be
made for this in a very rough and ready fashion. Data are given in Table 1.

Table 1: Revised income distribution 1969/70

Income group	Original[1]	Per capita	Revised I	Revised II
0- 20	6.9	8.6	7.9	7.9
20- 40	11.0	12.7	11.9	11.8
40- 60	15.2	16.4	15.0	14.9
60- 80	21.6	22.2	20.6	20.5
80- 90	15.5	14.1	14.6	14.4
90-100	29.8	25.9	29.9	30.4
Total	100	100	100	100

Source: Department of Census and Statistics, original data for the 1969/70
Socio-economic Survey.

[1] Relates to household; the other columns relate to persons.

One word on the various columns in Table 1. The column "original"
refers to the published data, ranked by household, irrespective of household
size. The column "per capita" readjusts these data to take account of varying household size. The column "Revised I" is calculated by "blowing up"
different income sources by different amounts. The final column is calculated
by removing an estimated number of domestic servants from the top decile,

[1] We know of one such series, for the USA in 1970; see US Department
of Commerce, Bureau of the Census, Current Population Reports, Consumer
Income, quoted in S. Jain, Size Distribution of Income, Compilation of Data,
IBRD, November 1974.

re-assigning them (arbitrarily) to the third decile from the bottom and
"bumping" the same absolute number of persons up from one decile to the next.

The final column "Revised II" comes closer than any other data source
we know to presenting an accurate picture of Sri Lanka's pre-tax and
subsidy income distribution. It suggests that the richest 10 per cent
of persons receive just over 30 per cent of total income, which, although
this figure is not in the table, is about 10 times the amount received
by the poorest 10 per cent of persons. This can be compared with the data
source mentioned for the USA, which shows the richest 10 per cent (decile)
of persons with 24.6 per cent of total income, the poorest 20 per cent
(quintile) with 6.7 per cent and the middle quintile with 17.4 per cent.

However, it is the shift from the "Per capita" column to the "Revised
I" which is most interesting. This was computed using estimates of under-
estimation suggested by Pyatt.[1] Wages and salaries were increased least
and rents and dividends most. The result was not only to increase the degree
of inequality substantially but to change radically the sources of income
of the rich and the poor. After revision the share of wage and salary income
of the poorest 20 per cent of persons rose from 47 per cent of their total
income to nearly 55 per cent. And the share of self-employment (profit)
income fell from 25 per cent to 17 per cent, i.e. the poor are revealed (if
these revisions are justified) as consisting far more of labourers and less
of self-employed persons than before. For the richest 10 per cent some
very different changes result. Wage and salary income drops from 51 per cent
to 32 per cent, rents and dividends rise from 3 per cent to 22 per cent and
self-employment income from 28 to 33 per cent. Thus the rich are shown to
be less composed of those with high salaries and more of those with large
property holdings.

By shifting from the "Per capita" column in Table 1 to the "Revised I"
column whole households were re-ranked. Table 2 shows the extent of movement
between old and new income groups. Thus 80.7 per cent of persons who were
in the poorest 10 per cent before income sources were re-weighted remained
in it afterwards. The share remaining in any quintile is naturally larger
than for any decile. In the middle ranges of the distribution approximately
one third remained in the same decile, one third moved up one decile and
one third moved down. There was least movement, however, out of the previously poorest and richest households.

---

[1] Suggested by G. Pyatt and A.R. Roe, Social Accounting for Development
Planning with Special Reference to Sri Lanka, Cambridge 1977.

Table 2: Share in former income group
who remain in new income
group (per cent)

Poorest decile	80.7
Poorest quintile	83.5
5th decile	33.7
Middle quintile	63.7
6th decile	32.7
Richest quintile	87.3
Richest decile	81.6

Source: Department of Census and
Statistics, op. cit.

This relative immobility at the top of the income range suggests
that alternative hypotheses on the importance of dividend income can be
suggested without too much abuse of realism. Thus, if there were no rents
and dividends paid at all the richest decile would enjoy an average income
some seven times that of the poorest decile (instead of ten times). Conversely, if all estates were owned within the country, and this doubled the
amount of rents and dividends received by the richest decile, their income
share would creep up to 35 per cent, some eleven times that of the poorest.

Taxation

Our discussion of income distribution so far has been carefully
phrased in terms of pre-tax income. This may, of course, be slightly decep-
tive since some "pre-tax" incomes are recorded after they have adjusted
themselves to anticipated levels of taxation. However, it is customary
to relate taxes to pre-tax incomes and to speak in terms of the incidence,
or the "burden", of perceived levels of taxation on certain income groups.
This is, in the Sri Lanka context, important since we have also referred
to the role of public financing in the provision of food and of welfare
services. It is, therefore, necessary to ask which income groups supplied
the bulk of tax income since, in its turn, tax revenue has supplied the
bulk of government income.

Here we shall draw largely on the work of P. Alailima of the Ministry
of Finance and Planning in her analysis of tax payments by income group in
1973.[1] Some slight changes have been made in order to put her findings on

---

[1] P. Alailima, "Fiscal Incidence in Sri Lanka", Geneva, ILO, 1978, World
Employment Programme research working paper (restricted).

to a quintile or decile base. The income distribution data used in her
analysis correspond to the second column of Table 1, i.e. to per capita
incomes using unrevised income data. The over-all tax burden (excluding
FEECs) amounted to some 13.2 per cent of household income, somewhat more
than the total cost of supplying free and subsidised food and other welfare
services. It is assumed in Alailima's analysis that income taxes are paid
by those legally liable to them and that export taxes are paid by producers.
Indirect taxes are assumed to be paid by consumers in proportion to their
expenditure on the taxed product in question (or to other final products
incorporating that taxed product). The results of this analysis are given
in Table 3. They show that the poorest 20 per cent were paying some 10.7
per cent of their income in tax, compared to a national average of 13.2
per cent. This calculation totals "Direct taxation" and "Indirect taxation".
The middle quintile pays 10.9 per cent and the richest 10 per cent pays 18.2
per cent. These results do not show a startling degree of progression (i.e.
bias in favour of the poor) although they are, in that sense, better than
results achieved for many other countries. Thus it has been similarly
calculated for the Philippines that the combined rate of direct and indirect
taxation is 26.4 per cent for the poorest quintile and 26.3 per cent for
the richest five per cent.[1]

Table 3: Distribution of the tax burden

	Direct taxation	Indirect taxation	Total taxation
Poorest 20	4.5	6.2	10.7
20 - 40	3.3	7.0	10.3
40 - 60	3.7	7.2	10.9
60 - 80	3.7	7.8	11.5
80 - 90	3.8	8.9	12.7
90 - 95	3.7	8.8	12.5
95 - 100	14.0	9.9	23.9
Average	5.4	7.8	13.2

Source: P. Alailima, "Fiscal Incidence in Sri Lanka", op. cit.

---

[1] See E. Tan, op. cit.

Monetary and non-monetary income in rural areas

The purpose of this brief section is to draw attention to the co-existence of both monetary and non-monetary income sources. This co-existence poses problems for the interpretation of household survey data and it is valuable to bring this matter out explicitly here. It must be remembered also that because a household makes some food sales at a certain point in time it is not necessarily a surplus producer. Storage problems and the liquidation of immediate debts can cause households to sell at one point of time and to buy back later. Bearing all this in mind Table 4 shows the major components of non-monetary income and their corresponding importance in money income.

Table 4: Rural (non-estate) income sources (per cent)

| | Income groups (Rs.) | | | | |
	0-100	101-199	200-299	400-599	600+
Non-monetary income in total income	28.6	22.3	17.5	15.0	13.3
Shares of non-monetary income					
Home produced:					
Housing	31.7	33.2	36.1	38.3	44.9
Cereals[1]	14.2	24.6	36.1	28.9	28.4
Coconuts and vegetables	26.9	18.3	16.0	14.9	12.9
Shares of money income					
Net income from:					
Cereals[2]	12.8	16.1	16.6	17.1	9.2
Coconuts and vegetables	1.2	2.0	1.0	1.2	1.6
Shares of total income					
Housing	9.0	7.4	6.3	5.7	5.9
Cereals	13.2	18.0	18.0	18.9	11.8
Coconuts and vegetables	1.6	1.6	0.8	1.0	1.4
Share of households in total	9.2	35.2	37.9	11.9	5.8

Source: Department of Census and Statistics, op. cit.

[1] Excluding the rice ration.

[2] Net profit income of paddy cultivators.

The data in Table 4 are useful in suggesting the likely effects of price shifts upon measured income distribution. A higher rice price will improve neither the distribution of non-monetary nor of total income. In

both cases rice provides a relatively low income share for the poorest
groups. In addition it is only those groups which sell more rice than they
purchase who will find their real living standards rise. A higher value
on housing will improve the over-all distribution of income and make
the distribution of non-monetary income more unequal. On the other hand,
higher prices for coconuts and vegetables, where the poor are likely to be
far closer to self-sufficiency than for rice, will improve both non-monetary
and total income distribution. However, the data also indicate one more
thing. Throughout the major range of rural households cereals provide a
fairly stable share of total income. Leaving aside the "real" effects,
i.e. that high cereal prices will only help those households which are
truly in surplus and that lower prices will reduce the command over alternative goods across the board, a rise or fall in cereal prices would make little
difference to measured rural income distribution whatever its effects on
the relation between rural and other sectors.

Broad income distribution trends

Of major interest, of course, are questions of how income distribution
in Sri Lanka has changed in the course of time. However, this discussion
has been pursued at length elsewhere.[1] Use has generally been made predominantly of the two Consumer Finance Surveys, of 1963 and 1973, conducted by
the Central Bank. It has already been mentioned that the coverage of these
surveys, on both the income and expenditure sides, fell significantly
between the two dates. It must be assumed that the bulk of this increase
in underreporting affected higher income groups. E. Lee has examined the
data of the surveys in detail and stressed points relating to those made
in our previous section, that differential price rises can have unexpected
effects and can certainly negate what otherwise seems a favourable trend in
income distribution. He raised very considerable doubt concerning the generally optimistic interpretation of data from the 1963 and 1973 surveys.

To Lee's discussion we would merely wish to add that 1973 was particularly unfortunate as the, only, choice for the terminal year because of the
food shortage and price rises at that time. In fact, particularly in rural
areas, the distribution of non-monetary income improved faster over the
period 1963-1973 than that of money income.[2] As noted earlier the most

---

[1] See E. Lee, "Rural Poverty in Sri Lanka", in ILO, *Poverty and Landlessnes*
In Rural Asia, Geneva 1977.

[2] The share of the poorest 40 per cent of spending units in money income
rose from 13.7 to 18.1 per cent and in non-money income from 16.4 to 23.9 per
cent. Note that in this calculation non-money income does **not** include the
value of the rice ration.

likely key to this phenomenon is a rise in relative prices not only of cereals, but of minor crops, e.g. coconuts, manioc, sweet potatoes and vegetables as well. In this respect 1973 saw a cut in the general level of the rice ration, and frequently uncertain deliveries (17 per cent less rice was distributed than in 1972). At the same time the level of output of manioc, a less desirable substitute, doubled. If both these phenomena mainly affected the poor their real living standard would probably fall, at least in their own eyes, but household surveys would record a rise in their incomes. If furthermore, all poor households were both sellers and buyers of manioc, both their non-monetary and their money incomes would rise.

Our intention here is, however, to escape from the detailed examination of survey results, rewarding although that may be when properly handled, and enter broader fields. In so doing we shall no doubt lose in detail. It will also be necessary to trespass to some extent on the subject matter of Chapter 5, "Structural features". It will be necessary to follow trends in prices, in the internal terms of trade and in earnings.

Price trends

Table 5 presents data on selected price movements from 1959. Firstly, it contrasts the implicit price deflator for manufacturing from the national income accounts with a series representing the evolution of producer rice prices. This series results from dividing the total of private expenditure and the net food subsidy on locally produced rice by paddy output. As such the series shows trends rather than reliable absolute prices. The table shows the constancy of average manufacturing prices from 1959 to 1968/69 compared to the jump in producer rice prices from 1965 to the end of the 1960s. However, by the mid-1970s the relative position was different again. Manufacturing prices were presumably strongly influenced by prices of imported intermediate goods which fell from 1959 to 1965 but rose very steeply in the 1970s. Industrial wages in large-scale industry which were apparently very constant in the early 1960s, rose very quickly in the 1970s. The Colombo consumer price index for food is also included, after changes have been made which are described elsewhere.[1] It should be noted that both the producer price of rice and the consumer food price index are strongly influenced by food subsidy policy, to which we shall return.

---

[1] See P. Richards, "A Note on Wages Policy in Sri Lanka", Bangkok, mimeo, 1974. This estimated the increase in food prices on the basis of the rise in domestic agricultural output (some 12 per cent for the period 1960-1973) and the increase in expenditure on foodstuffs.

Table 5: Price trends, selected statistics (1965 = 100)

	1959	1965	1968/69	1973	1976
1. Manufacturing	100	100	102	142	237
2. Imports, intermediate	110	100	122	230	488
3. Industrial wages	n.a.	100	n.a.	223	408
4. Imports, consumer	86	100	132	212	361
5. Producer rice price	n.a.	100	130	190	174
6. Consumer price, food	98	100	116	177 (est.)	217 (est.)
7. Consumer price, clothing	73	100	99	146	167

Source: Central Bank Reports, various.

1. Implicit price deflator of value-added in manufacturing.
2. Price index of imports of intermediate goods.
3. Average daily wages from Central Bank industrial statistics.
4. Price index of imports of consumer goods.
5. Total of private expenditure on rice and Government net food subsidy divided by domestic production.
6. Official price index until 1968/69. Data for the increase 1968-1973 were estimated in "A Note on Wages Policy in Sri Lanka", The increase from 1973-1976 is taken from the official index.
7. Official index.

The shift in the internal terms of trade in favour of rice production in the late 1960s (which was supported by the policy of selling imported wheat at a profit) took place during the period, probably, of fastest expansion in rice output. In principle, this increase in the profitability of agricultural assets, which almost certainly have always been extremely unequally distributed,[1] would have worsened rural income distribution. It seems indisputable that rural wages rose a great deal more slowly, under 50 per cent from 1965-1973, than did producer prices. In the late 1970s manufacturing prices began to rise faster than did agricultural (rice) prices. However, it is unlikely that the profitability of manufacturing rose at the same rate, given the increase in prices in imported intermediate goods and in wages. It is possible that public sector activity in manufacturing has had an effect in depressing price increases (and profitability increases). But what must be stressed here is the major role of the Government in determining the profitability of cereal growing through monopoly control of imports and through the particular means used to distribute those imports.

---

[1] Data on all assets of rural (non-estate) households were estimated in the Survey of Rural Indebtedness, 1957. This found that the richest 10 per cent of households held 56 per cent of all assets and the poorest 40 per cent had 4 per cent. The survey included land, housing, tools, etc.

Wages, earnings and profits

The next element to examine is that of shifts in wage differentials. Wages are shown in Table 6 in terms of multiples of rural wage earnings, the sources for which series are given in the notes to the table.   Data are given only up to 1973. This is largely because the basis for wage increases changed considerably after that date. In the early period, 1953-1963 the cost of living increase was slight and real rural wage earnings may have risen slightly, perhaps by nearly 10 per cent. In the second period the cost of living increase is estimated to have been some 65 per cent while rural wage earnings rose only some 40 per cent. (This rate of money increase tallies broadly with that given for average daily minimum wages for tea and rubber workers in the Sri Lanka Labour Gazette. However, the source of the data covers all agricultural workers.) The fall in real wages from 1963-1973 was fairly general (except for some urban unskilled and also clerical occupations), although in many cases it was made up in the period 1973-1976. In terms of the table an increase in differentials of 0.2 or 0.3 percentage points would be necessary to preserve real wages.

Table 6: Wage differentials (agricultural labour = 1)

	1953	1963	1973
Urban unskilled labour[1]	1.3	1.4	1.8
Government labour[2]	1.7	2.1	2.2
Government clerical[2]	3.2	3.3	3.1
Primary teacher[2]	2.7	3.6	3.7
Secondary teacher[2]	5.3	5.2	4.6
Engineering skilled labour[1]	2.0	3.2	2.8
Engineering unskilled labour	1.4	2.3	3.0
Clerical[1]	n.a.	3.4	3.8
Professional[1]	n.a.	4.2	4.1
Salesman[1]	n.a.	2.3	2.9
Doctor[2]	n.a.	5.8	5.3
Agricultural labour wage, Rs.[3]	52.0	58.0	80.0

Source: Central Bank, Surveys of Consumer Finances and Government Wage Scales.

[1] Average.

[2] Starting rates.

[3] 1973, average of main occupation earnings of tea estate workers and "other agricultural workers"; 1963 average main occupation earnings of "unskilled and semi-skilled labour" in rural and estate areas; 1953 calculated from 1963 level assuming a 10 per cent increase as for estate daily earnings.

Many of the wage series which go through from 1953 to 1973 show widening differentials, frequently the gap increases more quickly from 1953-1963 than later. In the second period differentials do not vary much. There is obviously a relative reduction in the higher incomes, or more correctly, in their starting rates, which may not be borne out by a comparison of average incomes (not available). However, some non-government urban workers, e.g. engineering unskilled, salesmen, increased their differentials while government clerical and labour grades at least held theirs steady. The conclusion must be that wages policy from 1953-1973 had no significant effects on reducing some of the most basic wage differentials.

Wages policy over the period had three major modes of expression; developments in public sector wages, private collective bargaining and the minimum wage of estate workers. This last has also been a major influence on earnings of non-estate farm labour in wet zone areas. The difference between monthly earnings of estate and non-estate rural workers in the 1963 and 1973 Consumer Finance Surveys is both small, some Rs. 5, and constant. While there were, and are, forms of earnings on estates in addition to the daily minimum, there is no evidence that they have increased faster than the minimum. Some of them, e.g. weeding contracts, probably diminished. The absence of structural change in the plantation sector, until nationalisation, will be discussed elsewhere. Suffice it to say that under the conditions on which the plantation sector generally operated constant real earnings were the best which could be expected, with almost certainly a declining standard of housing.[1]

The encouragement of collective bargaining was one of the objectives of the establishment of minimum wage boards. In some instances, of which engineering is the prime example, active union-employer bargaining was achieved by these boards. Another successful example of collective bargaining has been the Ceylon Mercantile Union. However, the bulk of wage earners outside the public sector have never been covered by collective bargaining and do not enjoy particularly favourable wage contracts and conditions of employment. Regulations under the minimum wage boards are so beset with exceptions that it is doubtful if they have had any significant effect on the trend of wages. However, even without the benefit of collective bargaining and union protection, many groups have preserved their real

---

[1] And, where estates were badly mismanaged, periods of severe poverty and under-nourishment. The current system of a price related bonus may have changed the picture, at least on better run estates.

incomes in the face of increased unemployment.[1]

This phenomenon of differentials being upheld despite higher levels of, particularly educated, unemployment applies strongly to the public sector. Average clerical earnings from 1963-1973 (including the private as well as the public sector) rose even faster than starting clerical rates (in the public sector). The 1971 ILO Comprehensive Employment Strategy Mission focussed on this very point and recommended a relative reduction in the salaries of white collar workers. However, while subsequent changes have brought starting clerical salaries closer to those of, at least, semi-skilled workers the career prospects for clerical workers are immeasurably better.

This piece-meal approach to wages policy, which, if anything was addressed to the preservation of differentials, lasted until the period of high inflation around 1973. Since then there has been the major new development of imposing across-the-board increases for anyone with any contract of employment, which were subsequently incorporated in minimum wages.[2] A 20 per cent increase was imposed in early 1974, 10 per cent in 1975, 6 per cent in 1976 and 25 per cent at the end of 1977. A further 10 per cent rise in late 1978 was not made obligatory on the private sector. All these increases, except the last, had absolute limits. Thus their relative effect was consistently greater for the poor than for the rich. This must be especially true in the public sector where the minimum starting rate in 1978 was Rs. 300. From 1973-1976, for the lowest paid these increases amounted to some 40 per cent while the cost of living rose some 20 per cent only. Over the period 1953-1976 this would probably have brought the real income changes of rural workers from negative to zero.

But we have looked so far solely at wage differentials. In addition we must consider other income sources and their interaction with wages and salaries. The major item to be considered here are the profits of resident companies. The incomes of resident companies assessed for tax in 1970

---

[1] And also preserved a high degree of job mobility, see P. Richards, "Job Mobility and Unemployment in the Ceylon Urban Labour Market", Oxford Bulletin of Economics and Statistics, Vol. 35, No. 1.

[2] Some collective bargaining agreements and minimum wage contracts also permit a cost of living increase. This is paid in addition to the imposed increase. These imposed increases are additive not multiplicative.

amounted to some Rs. 400 million and in 1972 to Rs. 612 million (compared
to Rs. 275 million in 1966).[1] These amounts are before tax, as are the
incomes compared under wage differentials. No precise data exist on the
amount of wage and salary payments in Sri Lanka with which to compare
this figure of company income.[2] The 1969/70 Socio-economic Survey showed
wages and salaries as 59 per cent of household income. They were earlier
estimated as 56 per cent of household income and 60 per cent of household
expenditure.[3] Since a series of private consumption expenditure data
exists wages and salaries are assumed to amount to 60 per cent of that
magnitude. For 1973 this gives some Rs. 7,300 million. Assessed
corporate income might be at least 8 per cent of this. Distribution
data from the Consumer Finance Survey shows that around two-thirds of
dividend income accrues to the richest 10 per cent of income receivers.
This is almost certainly an understatement and a truer figure would be over
90 per cent. No data exist on the distribution of wages and salaries
alone. In 1973 the average wage and salary must have been around Rs. 240
p.m. (i.e. three times rural-agricultural earnings). Average earnings of
the richest 10 per cent of wage and salary workers can only be guessed at,
Rs. 500 may be a fair estimate. (In which case the richest 10 per cent
of wage and salary receivers each would have an additional Rs. 125 per
month, i.e. each income would rise by one-quarter and the gap between richest
and poorest deciles rise from 6.2:1 to 7.8:1.[4] Since some of this company
income accrues to non-wage and salary earners this increase is exaggerated;
15 to 20 per cent may be a fairer figure. However, within the top 10 per
cent this income would be very unequally distributed and its contribution
to increasing differentials between, say, the richest 5 per cent and the
rest will be much greater.

---

[1] Not all of this income is distributed by any means (which is no
doubt one reason why share prices are low). Nevertheless it belongs to
shareholders.

[2] The Department of Census and Statistics publishes data on the share of
compensation of employees in national income. In each of the two series
available to us, for 1963-1968 and 1972-1976 the percentage was very stable,
at 48 per cent and 58 per cent respectively. The Statistical Abstract
gives 46 per cent for 1970. On this basis there was an apparent jump between
1970 and 1972 of 12 per cent. Without further investigation this increase
may merit scepticism.

[3] In Ministry of Planning and Economic Affairs, Economic Development
1966-68, Colombo 1967.

[4] This can be compared with the ratio of 10:1 for all incomes and all
persons given earlier.

Food subsidies

We have already drawn attention to the State's role in influencing cereal prices and the internal barter terms of trade. This occurs through the operation of the food subsidy which will be investigated here in more detail.

Table 7 gives some basic data on the operation of food subsidies on cereals since the mid and early 1960s. It should be explained that different political regimes have operated different food subsidy systems, as is, in fact, reflected in the ratio of the net food subsidy to the total of private consumption expenditure. From 1961/62 to 1965/66 this averaged some 5 per cent. For the next four years it averaged 3.4 per cent. In the early 1970s it reverted to around 5.4 per cent. These percentages hide a major shift in the attitude towards wheat imports. In the first period these were relatively small and more or less sold at cost price. They increased in size in the late 1960s when they were frequently sold at a profit, thus reducing the net food subsidy. In the early 1970s with the rise in world cereal prices wheat flour was sold at a considerable loss. However, the share of wheat flour in total cereal availability would appear to have remained fairly stable from the late 1960s to the late 1970s.

One is interested not only in the relation of the net food subsidy to total expenditure but in its distribution between income groups. Alailima's estimates for 1973 show the distribution of the subsidy as not as pro-poor as might be expected, although the rich certainly benefited from it less than in proportion to their numbers.[1] Nevertheless the benefit of the net food subsidy to rural workers would probably exceed that of the average. Given that the subsidy is per person it could well represent the equivalent of an additional 20 per cent on the earnings of rural workers. However, it must not be forgotten that the subsidy has in recent years operated increasingly through subsidising wheat flour, of which the rural poor consume less than average. Conversely the cut in the quantity of the rice subsidy in 1973 increased the amount of, unsubsidised, manioc produced in Sri Lanka from some 350,000 tons in 1970 to 750,000 tons in 1974. Even in 1970 the rural poor were consuming twice as much manioc as the average, i.e.

---

[1] P. Alailima, op. cit. The poorest 40 per cent of spending units received only some 31 per cent of the benefits. The system was, of course, changed at the end of 1977. It is possible that the sliding scale means test used at that time to "revalidate" ration books resulted in some anomalies. Note, however, that wheat flour is subsidised.

some 120 calories per person per day. By 1974 they may have been receiving at least 10 per cent of their total calorie intake from manioc.

Table.7: Food subsidy - selected data (per cent and Rs.)

	1962/63	1965/66	1968/69	1972/73	1975/76
1. NFS/private expd.	5.1	4.4	3.6	5.4	5.4
2. Govt/total expd. rice	n.a.	63	40	38	38
3. GPS + imp/total rice	72	80	45	53	47
4. GPS/domestic prod.	55	55	25	36	21
5. Wheat/all cereals	13	20	32	22	25
6. GPS + rice imp + wheat/cereals	76	84	63	63	60
7. Domestic prod - GPS/cereals	24	16	37	37	40
8. GPS price per bushel Rs.	12.0	12.0	14.0	14.0-18.0	33.0
9. Import price per bushel (FEECs) Rs.	11.5	12.7	19.1	23.7-66.2	46.0

Source: Central Bank Reports, various, also: H.N.S. Karunatillake, "Staff Studies" Central Bank of Ceylon, April 1975 and L. de Silva, "Staff Studies", April 1971.

1. Net Food Subsidy as share of private consumption expenditure.
2. Government subsidy for rice as share all expenditure on rice.
3. Government purchases of domestic rice production plus imports as share all rice consumed.
4. Government purchases as share domestic rice production.
5. Share of wheat flour consumed in total cereals.
6. Government domestic rice purchases plus wheat and rice imports as share all cereals consumed.
7. Share of domestic rice production not sold to Government in total cereal consumed.
8. Official price.
9. Converted from import prices using FEEC rate, i.e. plus 65 per cent.

The data in Table 7 must be seen in the light of the earlier figures showing the increase in producer prices. As the share of rice consumed passing through the government decreased after 1965/66, i.e. GPS purchases and rice imports, so the producer price of rice increased. Of course, the availability of wheat flour has placed a brake on the growth of rice prices. Hence the probable fall in producer prices despite the higher GPS price.[1] It is well to recognise the link between the availability of

---

[1] The role of GPS prices will be taken up again in Chapter 6. In 1973 producer prices were some way over GPS prices. In principle they cannot be below GPS prices, but they may be.

imports and domestic prices but it must also be recognised that imported
food could have been distributed in a different fashion, namely by being
freely available at a price which could have been dictated by the profitability of domestic production. It is a measure of the lack of political
influence of domestic rice producers that imported rice and wheat has been
for so long distributed at a low price.

The official purchasing price for domestic rice was raised to Rs. 12
per bushel in 1951 and stayed there until 1966/67. It was probably raised
to Rs. 12 as this was the equivalent of the then import price, which, at the
official exchange rate, subsequently fell and remained around Rs. 7 or 8
until 1966. However, the Rs. 12 price was not based on production costs
while the import price reflected more efficient production (in yields
per acre) or larger landholdings (and a lower profit per unit of output) in
exporting countries. However, GPS purchases by the government remained
high until 1967, reflecting the low level of demand outside the ration.

At a more realistic exchange rate (i.e. the old 65 per cent FEEC rate)
imported rice became relatively expensive from 1966 onwards, certainly up
to and including, 1976. Open market prices have, however, often exceeded
the GPS price particularly in the early 1970s and the share purchased has
fallen considerably.

Major factors in income distribution: a review

We can, at this stage, pick out a few of the major determinants of
income distribution in Sri Lanka. We have noted the relative position of
rural labour incomes, the strength and continuity of the relative differentials of clerical workers and urban organised labour but the fall,
relative to organised labour, of professional incomes. We have noted
the role of divident income which helps to preserve the income position,
inter alia, of many professionals. Conversely rents from domestic agriculture are almost certainly omitted from nearly all statistical sources.
The value and purchasing power of such rents almost certainly rose in line
with the shift in the internal terms of trade in favour of domestic agriculture. Agricultural labour and, no doubt, many tenants failed to gain
much benefit from this shift. However, the operation of the food subsidy
placed a limit on the rate of increase of domestic agricultural prices and,
by now, has probably pushed the internal terms of trade towards manufacturing.
Food subsidies have benefited organised labour although the extent of this
was much reduced by the changes made in early 1978 (revalidation of rice
ration books). Many poorer groups, however, failed to benefit proportionately

from the food subsidies since their consumption relied considerably on such
a non-subsidised staple as manioc.

CHAPTER 4

Poverty in Sri Lanka

Incomes and Poverty

Poverty in Sri Lanka has generally been approached in terms of income levels. We accept the validity of such an approach since income is the only measure of the diverse bundle of goods and services which are enjoyed by households. Nevertheless we have already noted the problems and confusions inherent in assessing welfare gains and losses through time based on a comparison of income levels. The Seers report considered, largely on the basis of the income required to purchase an adequate level of nutrition outside the rice ration, that "the income level of Rs. 200 per month per household may be taken as above the poverty line."[1] A rough and ready household poverty line of Rs. 300 per month for a 5 person household, rising by Rs. 60 for each additional person, was applied when ration books were revalidated. This level was chosen precisely in order to leave some 7 million people, or one half the population, below it.[2]

Poverty, it seems fair to say, consists in experiencing a whole bundle of undesirable circumstances. These circumstances can, of course, vary between different poverty groups. Under-nourishment may play a major role in one group, exposure to cold may be more important in another. In poor countries low incomes are a major indicator of the presence of certain serious poverty characteristics including hunger, or at least an unbalanced diet, income insecurity and probably indebtedness, absence of "cushioning" assets, poor living conditions, poor health etc. We have already discussed in Chapter 2 that in Sri Lanka income is a far less precise guide to the presence of many poverty characteristics than in other countries. Nevertheless those low income groups which are not effectively covered by welfare pro-grammes are experiencing a that much greater intensity of poverty.

We do not intend to construct an income cut-off point which will delineate poverty groups from the rest. Rather we shall investigate certain characteristics of those at the bottom of the income scale, paying

---

[1] See Matching Employment Opportunities and Expectations, A Programme of Action for Ceylon, ILO Geneva 1971.

[2] See Budget Speech 1978, given on 15.11.77. An income cut-off line of Rs. 300 might have been expected to have left substantially less than half the population below it. Later in 1978 an income cut-off point of Rs.500 pm was chosen for the operation of the income support scheme for the unemployed. Households with over five members can receive income support of Rs.50 pm for each of two unemployed members.

particular attention to their consumption, their employment and their unemployment. Firstly we shall simply point out which sectors have the largest shares of low income households. This is given in Table 1 which shows an incidence of low income households three times higher in the estate sector than in urban areas.[1] Given the low standard of many other facilities in estate areas and, an aspect not so far mentioned, the far less favourable climatic conditions particularly in Nuwara Eliya district, their poverty is, if anything, understated. But, the rural areas generally hold far more people than the estate areas. If we wish to look for the poor in rural areas the place to find them is among the same kind of people, labourers with small plots of land, as in estate areas.

Table 1: Incidence of low income households (per cent)

Household income	Urban	Rural	Estate	Total
0 - 99 (Rs.)	5.8	81.3	12.6	100
100 - 199 (Rs.)	8.6	73.4	18.0	100
(0 - 199) (Rs.)	8.1	74.9	17.0	100
All incomes	16.4	71.8	11.8	100

Source: Department of Census and Statistics, Socio-economic Survey, op. cit.

Poverty Characteristics

In Chapter 2, Table 5 demonstrated that average calorie consumption rises with income group. That table also would seem to indicate that in terms of calorie consumption there was virtually no poverty in Sri Lanka outside the urban areas, since elsewhere calorie intake was close to calorie requirements. An alternative interpretation might be that there was at that time very little systematic relation between under-nourishment and low incomes and that the desire to divert consumption to non-food items could be increasingly gratified with higher incomes. More detailed investigation of a sub-sample of the survey shows that relation between low incomes and low calorie intake is, in fact rather loose. In this sub-sample, of 197 rural households in Ratnapura, four measures, indicators of poverty

---

[1] i.e. comparing the sectoral share in one of the two low income groups to the same sector's over-all share. Rural and estate price levels are probably only 66-75 per cent of the urban level. This would tend to increase the incidence of urban poverty, but not by much.

characteristics, were available. These were income per capita (per person, not per equivalent adult), calorie consumption per adult equivalent, rooms per person and sanitary (toilet) facilities. The first three are available as distributional measures and in each case the "poorest", i.e. least favoured, quintile of households was identified. The fourth variable is not available as a distributional measure. However, as 29 per cent reported "no toilet facilities", this was taken as a measure equivalent to the others, which were all based on quintile distribution. There is, therefore, in this example, no attempt to set minimum levels, merely to compare the distribution of these four variables in order to assess the degree of overlap and to assess the distribution of any three indicators of poverty characteristics in terms of the fourth.

Table 2 gives the basic data in absolute numbers. Thus, e.g. of 38 households in the lowest per capita income class (quintile 1) 19 were in the lowest quintile of housing space, 18 had no toilet and 12 fell in the lowest quintile by calorie input. Reading from left to right shows in all but one case a steady reduction in poverty characteristics as per capita income rises. However, the lack of overlap between the lowest per capita income quintile and the lowest calorie consumption quintile is striking.

Table 2: Households with poverty characteristics

Households falling in lowest group for:	I	II	III	IV	V	Total
Total in quintile group	38	40	40	39	40	197
Calories	12	9	9	8	1	39
Sanitary	18	16	7	10	6	57
Rooms	19	6	6	4	3	38
Sum of 3 above	49	31	22	22	10	134

(Column header span: Income per capita, quintiles)

Source: Socio-economic Survey 1969/70, sub-sample 197 households rural Ratnapura.

Table 3 gives a different presentation. It shows that the poorest quintile by per capita income has 51 per cent of all poverty characteristics and the next poorest has 18 per cent. The next two quintiles have similar shares and the richest 20 per cent by income clearly has far fewer such poverty attributes. The table also shows that only 5 households experienced all four poverty attributes, compared to 109 households which experienced at least one such poverty characteristic.

Table 3: Household distribution of poverty indicators by income class

	Income per capita, quintiles				
	I	II	III	IV	V
Number of poverty indicators					
4	5[1] (20)[2]	-	-	-	-
3	10 (30)	-	-	-	-
2	14 (28)	7 (14)	2 (4)	5 (10)	-
1	9 (9)	17 (17)	18 (18)	12 (12)	10 (10)
Total	38 (87)	24 (31)	20 (22)	17 (22)	10 (10)
Distribution of characteristics					
Total 100	51	18	13	13	5

Source: Socio-economic Survey 1969/70, op. cit.

[1] Households with that number of poverty characteristics.
[2] Product of households and number of poverty characteristics.

Of the heads of the five households experiencing all the poverty characteristics all were male, all aged between 30 and 40, three were in paid employment, two self-employed, all engaged in undetermined activities. All the households fell into the least favoured 25 per cent in terms of dependency rates (adults aged 14+ to total household members). These findings suggest that a quick means of physically picking out the poorest households is to firstly look for the worst living conditions and then to check dependency rates.

Income Sources and Consumption

Unlike estate labour and the urban poor, the rural poor are in the position of producing some of their own food. They have what can be called a "food" income, consisting of sales of rice, vegetables etc. and of home consumption of the same products. For the rural areas as a whole, for example, the share of home produced rice in the total of non-ration rice consumed in 1969/70 was some 40 per cent while the share of home production in total coconut consumption was around 30 per cent.[1]

---

[1] For rice this percentage rises with income, for coconuts it generally falls.

Table 4 yields in this respect some very interesting and, for policy purposes, useful data on income sources of households of which the head was in a specified occupation. They show first of all, as might be expected, that paddy farmers' households receive a wage income while agricultural labourers' households receive a "food" income; the latter is generally more important than the former. In each case the importance of this alternative income source rises with income level. Poor rural workers are therefore more dependent on their major income source - wages and salaries - than are the better-off rural workers. Even on estates the importance of alternative "food" incomes rises with income group. It is thus clear that production for home consumption is by no means a substitute for low work incomes. Furthermore it is clear that low income workers' households are much more dependent on buying their food through the market than is any other (non-estate)group. The poorest rural workers' group has a non-monetary food income of some Rs. 5 (approximately 60 per cent of their "food" income). The richest rural workers' group has a non-monetary "food" income of Rs. 18 (under 30 per cent of their "food" income).

The data for housing and firewood can be taken as indicators not only of the amount owned (i.e. imputed rent) or supplied or collected free, but also of physical quantities used. This is because (i) very little rural housing is on rent, (ii) almost all estate housing is given free and (iii) most households collect their own firewood. In this respect the data in the "housing" column give an alternative and perhaps better measure of the welfare of the various groups. Income group for income group the paddy farmers come out best on this measure - which further suggests that, in fact, their total incomes may be the most underestimated of all. Otherwise the lowest income group on the estates scores more highly than the lowest income group of rural workers.

On the question of income underestimation it can be recalled that Chapter 3 described how various income sources had been given different weights. The effect of this was to worsen the relative income position of those households relying mainly on wage and salary incomes. This has the effect of shifting the incidence of poverty from cultivating households to labouring households.

As noted, in 1969-70 the share of home produced rice in total non-rationed rice consumed averaged 40 per cent and rose, although unsteadily,

Table 4: Source of rural and estate household income by income group of selected occupations, Rs. (and percentage)

	Wages	Food[1]	Housing[2]	Other	Total
Paddy culti-vators[3]					
Rs. 0 - 99	10.2 (12.7)	53.6 (67.0)	13.6 (17.0)	2.6 (3.3)	80.0
Rs. 100 - 199	19.5 (12.9)	108.3 (71.4)	17.1 (11.2)	6.6 (4.5)	151.5
Rs. 200+	59.9 (16.8)	254.2 (71.4)	28.3 (7.9)	13.3 (3.9)	355.7
Rural agri-cultural employees					
Rs. 0 - 99	58.5 (72.6)	8.2 (10.1)	9.6 (11.9)	4.3 (5.4)	80.6
Rs. 100 - 199	99.7 (68.1)	25.1 (17.1)	14.5 (9.9)	7.0 (4.9)	146.3
Rs. 200+	189.8 (63.8)	70.6 (23.7)	22.9 (7.7)	14.1 (4.8)	297.4
Estate agri-cultural employees					
Rs. 0 - 99	65.8 (82.4)	2.1 (2.6)	10.5 (13.1)	1.4 (1.9)	79.8
Rs. 100 - 199	127.3 (85.3)	4.7 (3.1)	13.3 (8.9)	4.0 (2.7)	149.3
Rs. 200+	250.1 (83.2)	17.2 (5.7)	20.6 (6.8)	12.5 (4.3)	300.4

Source: Socio-economic Survey, 1969/70.

[1] Includes items "profits" and "production for home consumption".

[2] Includes free housing (mainly estates), imputed rents and also imputed value of firewood collected.

[3] Rural.

NB. Percentages of each group in the occupational total are as follows:

	Paddy cultivators	Rural employees	Estate employees
Rs. 0 - 99	7.5	12.9	7.9
Rs. 100 - 199	36.6	52.0	54.9
Rs. 200+	55.9	35.1	37.2
Total	100	100	100

over the income range, to reach 79 per cent for the highest income group. Thus, while in fact the share of production for home consumption in total income falls as income rises the capacity of rural households to meet their subsistence needs, measured at least in terms of rice, rises along with income.

It can be calculated that for 1969-70 rural households in the income
categories up to Rs. 200, could not have been self-sufficient in foodstuffs. Their expenditure on foodstuffs averaged around 60 per cent of
total expenditure while (excluding free rice) their profits (i.e. largely
net sales of foodstuffs) and value of home production (and consumption)
never exceeded 50 per cent of income.[1] A wage income was thus necessary,
on average, not only to purchase non-foodstuffs but to cover the food deficit.
Even, therefore, if the poor on average would not need to sell food (as
they do because of the lack of storage space or the need to pay off debts)
they would still not have had sufficient. There is scope therefore for
policies both to increase their wage income and their food production.
Of course, however, the rural poor are not homogenous, and to their
occupational background we now turn.

Occupation of Low Income Rural Workers

Table 5 shows the occupational and employment status breakdown of
male workers aged 20-60 in rural areas.

The percentage split between employee and own-account worker was
much the same for the poor as for the whole rural area. This is, of
course, affected by the probable relative extent of under-estimation.
Looking first at own-account workers the poor clearly have a greater
dependence on agriculture, particularly for rice and vegetable cultivation. Interestingly enough smallholders in rubber, tea and coconuts
would seem fairly equally distributed among poor households and total
households. Low prices for plantation crops are not per se a cause of
relative rural poverty.

The industrial breakdown of rural employees shows much greater
differences between the low income groups and the total. The share of agricultural labourers (in non-estate areas) is far higher among low income
groups. Over one third of the lowest income group are agricultural
labourers. Conversely the over-all rural breakdown shows a far higher
percentage of employees in more "formal sectors" such as finance and
government, transport and communications (including the post office) and
even in trade and restaurants. The only non-agricultural sector where low
income earners are over-represented is food, beverages and tobacco manufacturing where traditional and low productivity techniques are most common.

---

[1] Even this calculation ignores the excess of consumption over income.

Table 5: Rural male workers age 20-40 by employment status and industry (per cent)[1]

	Employees[2]			Own Account Workers[2]		
	Income Group		All	Income Group		All
	I[3]	II[4]	Rural	I[3]	II[4]	Rural
Industry						
Paddy and Vegetables	10.4	9.2	7.1	29.6	28.8	24.9
Tea, Rubber and Coconut	16.4	14.5	8.3	1.0	1.1	1.1
Other Agriculture	7.5	4.6	3.1	2.8	2.8	2.4
Total Agriculture	34.3	28.3	18.5	33.4	32.7	28.4
Fishing	-	0.3	0.6	-	0.7	0.8
Food, Beverages and Tobacco	3.3	2.4	1.7	0.5	0.3	0.6
Other Manufacturing	2.4	4.9	5.5	0.5	0.3	0.6
Construction	2.3	3.2	3.4	0.5	0.7	0.6
Trade and Restaurants	1.9	3.5	4.5	3.3	3.2	4.8
Transport and Communications	0.9	2.0	6.0	-	0.3	0.5
Finance and Government	3.8	4.9	12.4	2.3	1.9	2.1
Unspecified	7.5	6.0	4.1	0.9	0.4	0.4
Total	56.3	55.5	57.0	41.8	43.2	40.7

Source: Socio-economic Survey.

[1] As per cent of all male workers in that income group; [2] In addition the share working as employers is as follows: income group I = 1.9, II = 1.3, All Rural = 2.3; [3] Household income = Rs. 0-100; [4] Household income = Rs. 100-20

It must be stressed that the industrial breakdown of the poor is much more heavily biassed towards tasks consuming high levels of energy than the rich. Nevertheless their food consumption, as has already been discussed, is relatively low.

Table 5 shows that some paddy cultivators are among the low income group. However it is a serious mistake to believe that paddy income accrues mainly to the poor. Data are strikingly deficient in this area but the best approximation is given in Table 6. This shows the distribution

of total "cereal income", i.e. the value of home consumption and the net
profit incomes of households whose heads gave "paddy cultivator" as
their occupation. The groups of households are ranked according to
total household income.

Table 6: Distribution of paddy income, 1969/70

Paddy-producing households	Share of total cereal income (per cent)	Cereal income per household (Rs.)
7.5	2.1	10.3
36.6	20.8	27.0
39.5	41.4	50.0
11.9	23.5	90.0
4.5	12.3	97.7
100.0	100.0	59.7

Employment, Hours and Earnings

If labour incomes are so important what information do we have on
hours worked and earnings? In this section we present some data on earnings,
hours worked and extra hours available of the employed in three broad,
wage-earning, occupations. It must first of all be stressed that surveys
of the type from which these data are drawn often attract incredible responses. Our data are presented after removing the 40 per cent of respondents in the sample who claimed a total of hours worked and extra hours
available for work of over 16 per day.

The data in Table 7 show rural labourers as having the greatest
share in the very short hours category and, indeed, in the two lowest
categories, i.e. over 30 per cent worked under 30 hours. Estate
labourers are more grouped, largely into the 31-52 hour range, than any
other category, with urban white collar workers following. Production
workers tend to have the largest share in the long hours categories. The
data on the extra hours for which respondents claimed they were available
for more work are generally higher for labourers than for production
workers and for production workers than for white collar workers. Income
is clearly important here. By and large there is an inverse relation
between hours worked and extra hours available. There are some exceptions
such as the shortest working group of estate workers who, on average, would

Table 7: Earnings, hours worked and hours available 1973 (hours per week)

Hours worked:	-10	11-30	31-44	45-52	53-63	64-69	70+	Total
Per cent of workers in each group								
Rural labourers	11.7	19.7	27.3	21.0	14.1	1.3	4.9	100
Urban labourers	3.1	18.5	29.2	26.2	16.9	-	6.2	100
Estate labourers	6.1	13.0	39.6	34.7	5.9	0.4	0.2	100
Rural production	6.7	12.2	26.3	25.8	19.8	1.6	7.6	100
Urban production	8.6	11.4	35.2	15.2	18.1	-	1.4	100
Urban white-collar	5.7	19.4	29.4	30.8	10.4	1.4	2.8	100
Extra hours available by group								
Rural labourers	19.0	19.0	8.6	3.3	1.3	-	1.0	
Urban labourers	24.0	10.8	6.2	3.5	-	n.a.	-	
Estate labourers	9.3	21.8	8.5	0.5	0.4	8.0	n.a.	
Rural production	10.6	14.7	7.1	1.3	2.0	3.4	-	
Urban production	14.0	11.2	3.8	-	0.7	n.a.	0.8	
Urban white-collar	8.8	7.0	2.0	2.3	3.4	-	-	
Hourly earnings by group (Rs.)								
Rural labourers	.37	.67	.56	.55	.50	.54	.46	
Urban labourers	.12	.63	.83	.68	.67	-	.58	
Estate labourers	.27	.50	.43	.39	.49	.36	-	
Rural production	.54	.89	.78	.84	.69	.77	.53	
Urban production	.07	1.26	1.15	1.18	.92	-	.46	
Urban white-collar	1.20	2.98	1.71	1.52	1.21	1.28	.76	

Source: Labour Force Participation Survey, Central Bank of Ceylon, 1973

appear to be genuine part-time workers, not available for a full week's work. In general, however, the labour groups which secured least work during the week were the most dissatisfied and wanted the greatest amount of additional work.

Turning to the data on hourly earnings it is clear that there is a fundamental difference between white-collar workers and all others. Once white-collar workers have reached the 11-30 weekly hours group their earnings begin to fall. For the other occupations the general rule is for earnings to stay fairly steady and only fall once a very high number of hours are completed. For labourers there is little difference in hourly

earnings between, say, the 11-30 hour group and the 53-63 hour group.
Production workers are in a slightly intermediate position with obviously
an element in their wage invariant with respect to hours. It is interesting to note that in every case those who worked under 10 hours were
earning the lowest hourly wage. There is obviously a threshold within the
11-30 hour range after which a short time worker at least receives the
hourly pay normal for his sector and occupation. Workers below that threshold
are doubly disadvantaged, in hours and in pay. The hourly data finally
clearly show that working more hours has little negative effect on hourly
earnings for labourers. More work is obviously a means of supplying more
income.

Unemployment

It is time to bring in a discussion of unemployment in Sri Lanka
and its relation to poverty. Here we concentrate on the unemployed
in the age groups 15-19, 20-24 and 25-29, their household per capita income
and their education characteristics as revealed by the 1969/70 Socio-
economic Survey. The unemployed in these age groups account for nearly two-
thirds of the total. Furthermore we assume that for younger age groups
household income is largely determined by the employment status of older
people. Unemployment in older age groups is likely to be associated with
poverty, ipso facto. It has frequently been stated that unemployment in
Sri Lanka is predominantly a problem for the educated and thence reasoned
that unemployment may weigh more heavily on labour force members from rich
than from poor families. This reasoning is true in this respect only, that
the highest unemployment rates for any age-education group are generally
associated with the highest education levels. As Table 8 shows, up to 50
per cent of those qualified to "O" level and above in the 20-24 age group
in particular are unemployed. But, on the other hand, people with these
qualifications do not predominate among the unemployed. Only among female
unemployed in the older age groups and from the richer households (and
among males aged 25-29 from the richest household group) does this educational category form a majority. Generally the middle education groups
predominate. Those with no schooling form up to 10 per cent of total
unemployment among 15-19 year old females in the poorest groups but generally
their share is insignificant.

In fact, far from open unemployment weighing most heavily on the rich,
the data indicate that it weighs most heavily on the poor, for a number of

Table 8: Unemployment as a percentage of population for each age and education group

Income group	Age 15-19 Education level[1]				Age 20-24 Education level				Age 25-29 Education level			
	1	2	3	4	1	2	3	4	1	2	3	4
					Males							
I	39	34	22	31	18	20	35	40	-	10	24	35
II	15	31	24	35	27	20	40	51	2	2	20	23
III	21	19	16	16	-	10	35	43	8	3	10	7
IV	18	21	18	33	8	9	22	40	8	5	9	11
V	7	9	11	16	3	8	26	31	7	3	8	13
					Females							
I	8	9	8	20	3	14	20	57	1	-	9	-
II	13	8	9	32	4	4	16	43	-	1	11	19
III	9	7	8	24	2	3	14	51	4	1	5	49
IV	-	6	8	31	2	1	15	40	-	2	10	30
V	-	4	4	21	1	3	10	30	-	2	4	17

Source: Department of Census and Statistics, Socio-economic Survey, op. cit.

[1] 1 = no schooling; 2 = primary school; 3 = middle school; 4 = "O" level and above.

reasons. For the composite 15-29 age group unemployment rates (as a share of population) fall consistently from the poorest to the richest per capita income quintile for males as shown in Table 9.[1] Unemployment for females displays a somewhat different pattern with remarkable stability of rates for the 15-29 age group across income groups. When broken down into the three age groups the poor have generally the highest unemployment rates for males although not for females. But, on the other hand, the poor unemployed are much younger than the rich unemployed, largely, of course, because they leave school earlier. Fully 62 per cent of males unemployed from the poorest households in the 15-29 age group are between 15 and 19, compared to only 24 per cent of those from the richest household group.

---

[1] Other investigators have found little relation between unemployment rates and household income. It is the use of per capita income which changes the picture. For any level of household income, the larger the household the lower will be its per capita income and the greater the number of persons in the unemployment-prone age groups.

Table 9: Employment and unemployment rates

	Unemployed/population				Employed/population				Age structure unemployed			
	15-19	20-24	25-29	Average	15-19	20-24	25-29	Average	15-19	20-24	25-29	Total
						Males						
I	28	28	15	26	29	61	81	45	62	31	7	100
II	26	32	10	25	34	62	88	53	52	41	7	100
III	17	26	6	18	33	67	92	59	40	52	8	100
IV	20	21	8	17	31	71	89	61	42	46	12	100
V	11	24	9	15	30	63	88	60	24	58	18	100
						Females						
I	9	19	2	10	13	25	32	20	47	50	3	100
II	11	14	5	10	16	28	30	23	44	44	12	100
III	9	14	8	10	15	24	24	20	36	46	18	100
IV	9	15	10	12	16	23	24	21	29	49	22	100
V	7	15	8	10	13	20	21	18	23	56	21	100

Source: Department of Census and Statistics, Socio-economic Survey, op. cit.

While they leave school earlier, on average, the poor are not necessarily more likely to be employed than the rich. Rates of employed to
population in each household income group given in Table 9 show that, among
males, the poor have consistently the lowest rate (not that the rich have
the highest rate). Among the females the position is not the same and in
the 25-29 age group the poor are in fact much more likely to be employed
than the rich. This difficulty for the poor to find employment seems, for
males at least, to hold whatever their level of education. Table 8 showed,
for example, that for males in the age group 25-29 of those with "0"
level and above 35 per cent from the poorest households were unemployed,
compared to 13 per cent from the richest households. More surprisingly, in
the 15-19 age group the poor had the highest unemployment rates for males
for those with no or only primary schooling. Among females the position
is again not quite the same and unemployment rates by age and education show
a more mixed pattern.

The general picture that emerges is that the poor have higher unemployment rates, that more of their unemployed are young, that the rich
unemployed are more educated and that, whatever their level of education
the poor have greater difficulty in finding employment. This is the main

picture of male unemployment; female unemployment is distinguished by a
greater age and education spread between income groups but by an over-
all less unsatisfactory position for the poor. Female unemployment most
certainly does not weigh most heavily on the poor. Given the average
female unemployment rate of 10 per cent for both the richest and the
poorest group the income foregone by the richest groups is likely to considerably exceed that of the poorest.

Income foregone can be estimated in terms of relative earnings by
education group of young workers. Of course, the inter-educational group
spread of young workers' earnings is less than that of older workers. If
unemployment in youth has a marked effect on the pattern of later
earnings these relative earnings will understate the income cost of educated unemployment.[1]

On this basis of calculation the average income foregone per female
unemployed is some 27 per cent higher for the rich than the poor. In
fact, a very similar figure applies to males, but, on the other hand, the
poorest households have 70 per cent more unemployed than the richest
households. Averaging for both males and females the income foregone per
person unemployed is 27 per cent higher for the richest than the poorest
households while the latter have 35 per cent more unemployed. This
finding indicates that any unemployment is likely to hurt the poor more
than the rich and that any move towards full employment should benefit the
poor more than the rich. If the absolute weight of unemployment measured
in income terms is greater for the poor then the relative weight is many
times greater. The provision of more jobs for the 15-24 age group, in
particular jobs not requiring any great skill level, will help the poor.

Access of the poor to work and land: rural labour

We noted above that particularly in rural areas the poor can be helped
both by working on factors determining the level of the wage income and by
improving their access to land. In this section and the next we therefore
look first at rural labour then at estate labour. The last section looks
at land access both in terms of expanding existing villages and in terms of
encroaching into dry zone areas.

Low income rural groups are particularly dependent on a wage income.
We can therefore investigate the major forces determining that income particularly in agriculture. On the demand side there are the twin elements of
an unequal distribution of farmland and of a high degree of seasonality
in rice production. This element of seasonality may have been

---

[1] The earnings used here, for both males and females, are Rs. 70,
Rs. 104, Rs. 158 and Rs. 205 in ascending order of educational qualifications,
respectively.

sharpened by the use of **new rice** technologies. The demand for hired labour
therefore arises partly because family labour is insufficient, a situation
which may be worsened by the unwillingness of some educated youth to assist
their families, and partly because of high peak period labour needs. In the
newly opened areas of the Dry Zone family labour appears generally insufficient, thus giving rise to considerable internal seasonal migration. On
the other hand cultivation peaks in the Wet and Dry Zones do not coincide
exactly.

On the supply side most Wet Zone villages have a sizeable group of
"landless", people that is with no current access to agricultural land.
Village surveys have shown that this landless group may well include 50
per cent of the labour force.[1] This group has little alternative but to
offer to work for others. Even where crown land is available for encroachment as in the Dry Zone, the labourers are unable to find the initial capital
to finance cultivation. And even if they do they have to find some form of
wage employment to feed their families until harvest time. Such labourers
prefer casual work in agriculture with daily wages to permanent work such as
road construction with monthly wages. Daily earnings help them to meet their
immediate food and medical expenses.

Non-cultivation of paddy lands due to crop failure and bad weather
compels many farmers in the rainfed Dry Zone areas to work as casual agricultural labourers to meet their family food requirements. During the
1972-1976 period when large parts of the Dry Zone were affected by drought
many farmers (most of them by no means landless) moved to large colonisation
schemes in search of casual work or worked in the chenas opened up by big
time farmers.

Some cultivators and self employed also hire out their labour (especially
seasonally) to supplement their incomes. This group accounts for a considerable proportion of casual and part-time labourers. Their objective
is not only additional income for subsistence but also additional working
capital for their own enterprises. The large scale migration from Wet Zone
villages to Dry Zone colonisation schemes for seasonal work is noteworthy here.

---

[1] R.D. Wanigaratne, W. Gooneratne and N. Shunmugaratnum, "Administration
of land reform implementation in Sri Lanka: case studies", 1978, paper
prepared for the Asian and Pacific Development Administration Centre,
Kuala Lumpur.

Rural labour is by no means a homogenous category. Apart from age and sex differences labourers from certain areas are traditionally regarded as more efficient for some paddy operations. Labourers from parts of Kurunegala, Kegalle and Matale are employed (mostly in land preparation, transplanting and harvesting) in the Dry Zone at much higher wage rates than in the Wet Zone. Male labourers from certain muslim groups in the Samanturai-Kalmunai areas are thought better than females in reaping paddy, something done mostly by females in other areas.

The relations between labourer and employer are rarely clear cut. Landless labourers often borrow money from farmers for consumption. Small farmers sometimes borrow from big landlords for cultivation. These loans may be repaid by supplying labour. In such ways employers assure themselves of a regular "clientele" of labourers who, wanting to maintain good relations, may not ask for higher wages or work elsewhere at a higher wage. Sometimes the most popular client becomes a labour intermediary supplying labourers to the employer at a prenegotiated wage rate. In this way, quasi-permanent groups of labourers emerge to work with a particular employer.

Participation in social functions further strengthens patron-client relationships. Labourers may work free at the employers' house during weddings, funerals, etc. to show their attachment. The employer usually does not participate in the labourers' social functions but sends money or gifts. For migrant work on colonisation schemes, however, recruitment is mostly through intermediaries. The intermediary contracts with the farmer to complete certain operations such as harvesting etc. within a specified time period. He hires individual casual labourers or labour gangs paid per day.

It must also be recognised that in areas of acute land scarcity and over-population the position of tenants and labourers tends to approximate. Where the landowner takes a 50 per cent rent share and charges for other inputs the tenant may indeed receive a net return per day worked which is less than the current wage rate. In addition, of course, he has to take a number of risks himself. One system worth noting here is that of hired farmers who are really unregistered tenants. They are hired by resident landlords or their agents. The hired farmer is responsible for all aspects of production until the transport of produce to the agent's house. One eighth of the total harvest is first given to the landlord. Then expenses for inputs supplied by the agent are reimbursed from the balance. The rest of the harvest is divided into two equal parts with one given to the agent.[1] For the hired-farmer, the system is likely to be more disadvantageous than supplying casual labour.

In the South-west and Central regions, where population pressure on available paddy land is acute, most share tenants appear to be registered as hired labourers in the Paddy Lands Register. However, they are not paid daily wages and in fact are "under-hand tenants".

It is generally believed that the spread of new high yielding varieties of rice has created a demand for more labour. Data confirm that in the Dry Zone, where the adoption of NHYVs of rice was widespread, especially in areas of assured water supply,[2] the total amount of labour use per acre has increased. For example, in Polonnaruwa 68 mandays per acre were used in 1972. This increased to about 92 mandays in 1976/77. In Hambantota, labour use per acre was 40.6 mandays in 1972 and 50.7 in 1976/77.[3] These increases can be attributed mainly to more labour intensive operations, such as transplanting, which came into being with the NHYVs. Moreover, the increase in yields per acre has also contributed to higher labour use in harvesting and threshing. However, the use of hired labour shows only a slight increase. Hired labour increased only by 3 mandays in Polonnaruwa and by 4 mandays in Hambantota between 1972 and 1976/77.

Mechanisation of paddy cultivation in Sri Lanka took place much before the introduction of high yielding varieties. Tractorisation has been confined more or less exclusively to the Dry Zone. In some districts tractors have mainly replaced buffaloes, while in others they replaced both buffaloes and human labour. Human labour is of course necessary to work with tractors. In fact this labour requirement may even be higher since without tractors many acres of the Dry Zone would have to be left fallow each year. However, it would not appear that mechanisation has significantly affected labour needs.

The impact of technological change on rural wages remains even less clear. Data suggest that money wages have increased mainly in the Dry Zone districts where technological change has taken place rapidly.

---

[1] Jayantha Perera, "A Study of Socio-economic Conditions of Agricultural Labour in Sri Lanka - Preliminary Observations and Findings", 1977 (mimeo.).

[2] In areas served by minor tanks water supply is extremely erratic.

[3] K. Izumi and A.S. Ranatunga, "Cost of Production of Paddy, Yala 1972", 1973, ARTI Colombo, Research Study Series: 1.

All in all the weak economic status of rural labourers has prevented the growth of their bargaining power. Formal labour organisations are absent in rural areas unlike in towns and estates. The absence of rural trade unionism has several causes. Firstly, different categories of labourers have different interests. Common interest is lacking. Secondly, employers in rural areas generally enjoy a higher socio-economic and political position, and can easily use their greater access to police and political power groups to prevent the formation of labourers' organisations. Thirdly, the left-wing political parties which led the collective action of the urban and estate workers in Sri Lanka never had the same power base in rural areas. The rural people, being conservative in nature, have mainly supported the other political parties.

Absence of formal (or registered) labour unions does not necessarily suggest that there are no "informal labour organisations" in the rural sector. Informal labour organisations include ad hoc groups of labour which are not registered with the Labour Department as trade unions and are formed for some specific purpose. They also include informal gatherings of individual labourers. Such informal organisations may exist but reported information is meagre. Wickremasekera reports two instances where groups of labourers in a Dry Zone village and in a Wet Zone village organised protests successfully to get their wages increased.[1] Harris mentions an "Agricultural Labourer and Tenants Union" set up by a group of young men, which had some success in protecting tenant farmers in a village in the Hambantota district.[2]

Estate Labour

The next major group to be considered in this chapter is that of estate labour. Like rural labour they are dependent on a wage income but so many features differentiate the two groups. Estate labour is immobile, but unionised and the subject of considerable legislation imposing certain standards on employers. Its minimum daily wage is fixed by a wages board,

---

[1] Piyasiri Wickramasekera, "Aspects of the Hired Labour Situation in Rural Sri Lanka, Some Preliminary Findings", in S. Hirashima (ed.), Hired Labour in Rural Asia, Institute of Developing Economies, Tokyo, 1977.

[2] John Harris, "Social Implications of Changes in Agriculture in Hambantota District", in B.H. Farmer (ed.), Green Revolution? Technology and Change in Rice Growing Areas of Tamil Nadu and Sri Lanka, Macmillan London, 1977.

and its relation to its employer, the Superintendent, the plantation
company or now the State is contractual and impersonal. Like some forms
of rural labour recruitment originally centred around a gang boss, or
Kangany, who continued as the first level supervisor, and in the past was
often able to exploit his position profitably through loans and overcharging
in any goods he might have a hand in selling. Indebtedness was indeed one
of the first objects of attack of the All Ceylon Estate Labour Federation
founded in 1931. The role of intermediary is now increasingly taken over
by a union official, the thalaivar.[1]

Unemployment among estate workers gathered momentum in the 1950s and
1960s. The estate population grew while commodity prices fell. Although
in some parts of the estate sector profits remained high, re-investment
was slow and labour requirements stagnated. Yields in all three major
plantation crops stagnated. Estate management preferred to offer a
reasonable number of days work to existing labourers so that the labourers'
children were frequently not taken on to the check lists. Mobility within
the estate sector virtually dried up. Movement out of the estate sector,
despite the availability of certain jobs,[2] was meagre. For this there
are many reasons, the different ethnic background of so many labourers,
their non-citizenship, their consequent fear of harassment and the absence
of an ordinary rice ration book (rather than a card entitling the labourer
to a ration supplied through the estate) are all important features.
At the same time repatriation, which had been fairly common during the 1930s,
slowed down, the Government of India refused to accept estate labourers as
Indian citizens and it required the 1964 Indo-Ceylon agreement
(Sirima-Shastri pact) to iron out international obstacles. After the pact,
however, the majority of those eligible for Indian citizenship still
opted to remain in Sri Lanka and the proportions laid down in the pact,
i.e. 4 persons to be given Ceylon citizenship for every 7 given Indian
citizenship, slowed down repatriation again. More recently, perhaps
because of increased communalist fears, repatriation would appear to
have speeded up.

The totally dependent position of estate labour was effectively
acknowledged early on by a series of official ordinances laying down the

---

[1] See, Dr. K. Jayawardene, "Basic Needs, Workers' Organisations
and Labour Policies in the Plantation Sector", paper presented at the
joint ILO-ARTEP and ARTI Seminar on Employment, Resource Mobilization and
Basic Needs through Local Level Planning, Colombo, 1979.

[2] e.g. toddy-tapping, as discussed in ILO, Matching Employment Opportunities
and Expectations, A Programme of Action for Ceylon, Geneva, 1971.

areas of responsibility of estate managements. These included the Diseases
Ordinance of 1912, covering housing and health services, the Education
Ordinance of 1920 enforcing elementary vernacular education for children,
the Workmen's Compensation Ordinance of 1934 and the Maternity Benefits
Ordinance of 1939. But clearly, however effective such legislation was
in the 1930s, it has totally failed to provide the same level of welfare
on estates in the 1960s and 1970s as is enjoyed outside.

One other such piece of legislation was the Minimum Wage Ordinance of
1927 which required payment equivalent to the minimum wage if work was not
available for 6 days in the week. This has remained a dead letter
and work has commonly been available for 20 days per month at the most.
The consequent degree of un- and underemployment, the risk of a total disruption in work from e.g. the uncertainty arising from estate sales and
transfers and the possibility of estates (under their previous management)
being gradually run down all conspired to make the position of estate labour
as unfavourable as possible.

Against this background the two major estate labour unions have had a
hard struggle. Unions were originally strongly opposed by the plantation
management which for long was able to prevent union meetings on estate
land. But although these two unions, the Ceylon Workers Congress (with
over 100,000 due paying members) and the Democratic Workers Congress
(with some 45,000) are the largest in the country they can act only on
day-to-day matters. They have their political affiliations but have exerted
little political muscle. However, in many ways the situation is changing.
As more Indian tamils become citizens and more Sinhalese take up work,
but not necessarily residence, on estates the degree of alienation of estate
labour will no doubt fall. Conversely, however, the unanimity of interest
which was perhaps estate labour's only strength in the past, may be
diminished.

Access to Land

A major factor determining access to new land in Sri Lanka is the 1840
Waste Lands Ordinance. Under this measure all uncultivated land passed
into the hands of the State, some of it, of course, to be sold to foreign
and, later, local planting interests. However, the State thereby took
large tracts of unsettled dry zone land under its control so that any
expansion of cultivation required official permission and any group of
cultivators became encroachers until their position was regularised. The
law is still implemented but the last fifty years have witnessed fast
increasing flexibility and willingness to recognise the rights of
encroachers even on otherwise reserved land. Since the 1930s the

administration has recognised the importance of providing additional land simply to cater for the immediate needs of expanding village populations. Moore and Perera [1] report that by 1970 some 580,000 allotees had been settled on an average of 1.33 acres each under village expansion schemes. Some 55,000 allottees had received about six-tenths of an acre each from acquired estate lands. Since all unused land belongs to the State no village expansion can take place without bureaucratic involvement.

While some village expansion may have begun through encroachment this phenomenon applies more to remoter dry zone lands, and is generally for cultivation rather than homestead plus home garden purposes.

Data on encroachments are by no means accurate as official documents describe only detected encroachments. As the end of 1977 there were 178,741 acres of encroached lands in the country with 110,640 units. Almost 72 percent of this extent was in 8 Dry Zone districts. Even this official figure shows that the number of encroachers is much higher than that settled under State sponsored colonization schemes since the early 1940s. The example of the Gal Oya Scheme in the 1960s illustrates the rate of encroachment.

Table 10: Gal Oya: Settlers and Encroachers

	No. of Colonists Settled	No. of Encroachers
1963/64	292	378
1964/65	933	1,107
1965/66	100	600

Source - Annual Reports, Gal Oya Development Board.

Village expansion schemes can by no means provide a sufficiently large land holding to bring in even a subsistence income. Such schemes are, in any event, likely to occupy generally undesirable land, steep, rocky or waterless. Had it been good land it would no doubt have been cultivated earlier. The new lands are generally further from roads, schools and buses.

[1] M.P. Moore and Jayantha Perera, "Land policy and village expansion in Sri Lanka", Marga, Vol. 5, No. 1, 1978.

Moore and Perera, however, describe more specific drawbacks of village expansion. The allottees must by definition be landless and poor to qualify. Better-off village households have in any case no incentive to move away from their more conveniently situated home village. Furthermore the allottees are often those villagers whom the local leadership finds troublesome. As a result the allottees (local colonists) have no power or influence and no higher status leaders to plead for them. Since they are all poor they can do little to help each other. The results are frequently anti-social behaviour, violence and no mitigation of poverty.

Dry zone encroachment, however, is likely to be more individual and independent. Although landless people from the Purana villages of the Dry Zone have themselves encroached on considerable extents of land, the majority of encroachers have come from the Wet Zone. Eradication of malaria, improved physical access and the spread of educational and medical facilities following the establishment of colonisation schemes have been more responsible for exerting a pull towards the Dry Zone than the push factors such as landlessness, unemployment and poverty in the Wet Zone. Indeed the cities have, for various reasons, lagged behind the Dry Zone in exerting a strong pull effect. Opening of the Dry Zone through the expensive resettlement programmes has indirectly propelled the wave of spontaneous settlement. And, in the absence of a food subsidy, it is doubtful that such large numbers would have moved to the Dry Zone to practice highly risky rainfed cultivation.

The State has had little direct concern with encroacher communities except for its administrative involvement in detecting, evicting or regularising the occupants. The attitude of the State has, in general, been sympathetic, and most genuine land seekers are finally regularised, but it has certainly been far from constructive. Nevertheless encroachers today contribute substantially to the country's food production, especially in highland crops.

Compared with the colony settlers and the Purana villagers, the encroachers are placed at both an economic and a social disadvantage. They lack organised community life for encroachments, by necessity, take place in an unorganised form and on locations away from established settlements. Hence, they have little access to such welfare facilities as transport, education and health, as shown below for Uda Walawe.

Table 11: Uda Walawe Encroachers, Distance to Service Facilities
per cent of households

	- 2 miles	2 - 4 miles	Over 4 miles	Total
Dispensary	28	37	35	100
Hospital	7	25	68	100
Primary School	41	33	26	100

Source   Survey of Encroachers in Uda Walawe, Department of
Geography, Colombo University, 1976 (data supplied
by Dr. P. Silva).

Secondly, the encroachers benefit least from government agricultural
programmes. With no land title they are excluded from institutional
credit while the cooperatives which supply other inputs are located too
far away. Most encroachers mainly cultivate highland food crops (grains,
pulses, vegetables, chillies etc.). Generally there are no incentive
prices for these. Remoteness makes marketing a serious problem. As
a result encroachers are tied to private creditors and merchants to
obtain loans and to dispose of their produce. Agricultural extension services
rarely reach this group.

With no certainty they will retain their land, relying solely on
the rains and with no benefits from government programmes few of them
(only 13 per cent in Uda Walawe) had other assets such as livestock
and almost 50 per cent had to supplement their incomes by working as
agricultural labourers. School attendance of children of encroacher
families is very low; housing is extremely poor; 95 per cent of encroacher
families in Uda Walawe live in crude wattle and daub houses with a thatched
roof. These are the conditions under which the poor have ready access
to Dry Zone land.

Organised action to improve the lot of this clearly disadvantaged
group has been minimal, partly due to their diverse origins and partly
because speedy regularisation depends largely on an individual's ability
to influence politicians and state officers. Clearly, this is a group
that must evolve into organised communities and be integrated into the
agricultural and rural development programmes of other rural areas.

PART III: CHAPTER 5
                    Structural Features and Structural Changes

Introduction

The aim of this chapter, which itself constitutes a separate part of
the study, is to examine certain phenomena which provide the background to
recent economic and social policies in Sri Lanka. Most of these are directly or indirectly the result of government policies. Thus structural change
on estates, which we separate into pre and post-land reform, has always been
susceptible to possible government intervention. The same naturally applies
to the structure of employment and value-added, to foreign trade and obviously to the pattern of government investment. It is the very stability of
government action in certain areas which makes all the more interesting the
abrupt changes which were introduced, such as land reform for example. Other
shifts have been more gradual such as government intervention in manufacturing,
where we summarise the position in the early 1970s. We begin with a discussion of the pattern of government investment and with changes in some
major components of foreign trade. We then move to structural change in
rural and, pre-land reform, estate areas. We follow this with a discussion
of changes outside agriculture and present over-all data on value-added and
employment. We finally discuss the land reform of 1972 and 1975.

Government investment in productive assets

In Table 1 we have taken government investment in productive assets as
the total of government capital expenditure (on economic services) and government capital transfers. The latter represent largely grants to public corporations for the purchase of transport equipment and machinery or for land
and irrigation development. Our calculations unavoidably exclude the investment of public corporations from their own resources. Since they cannot
raise their own loans, such resources would be either current income or, possibly, bank advances. Nevertheless on our definition the government, which is
then not quite equivalent to the public sector, has in recent years controlled
between two-thirds and four-fifths of total productive investment. As a share
of GNP this investment rose from around 4 per cent in 1963 to between 6 and 7
per cent in recent years. Government investment has been dominated by its
three major components throughout the period; communications, which includes
transport equipment; agriculture and irrigation and manufacturing. Agriculture and irrigation has remained the major single component, accounting for
some 2 per cent of GNP. It is this sizeable portion of government investment
which has financed land development in the Dry Zone. The portion spent on

manufacturing, up to some 1.5 per cent of GNP, has been the motivating force behind public ownership of new large-scale enterprises.

Public control of such a large share of total productive investment has given successive governments considerable power to direct the development of the economy. Nevertheless looking solely at the pattern of this investment suggests that few changes have been made in the use of those resources.

Table 1: Structure of government capital expenditure and capital transfers (per cent)

		1963	1968	1973	1975	1977
I.	Investment in productive assets as share GDFCF[1]	62.0	55.0	46.0	56.0	56.0
II.	Govt. investment as share of I	40.0	73.8	68.5	79.2	66.3
III.	II as share of GNP	4.0	6.9	5.6	7.2	5.9
IV.	Major components of Govt. investment:					
	i. Communications	20.0	24.0	27.0	27.0	23.0
	ii. Agriculture and irrigation	51.0	33.0	35.0	34.0	29.0
	iii. Manufacturing	27.0	23.0	15.0	19.0	27.0
	iv. Other	2.0	20.0	23.0	20.0	21.0

Source: Department of Census and Statistics, National Accounts of Sri Lanka, 1970-1977, Colombo 1978 and Central Bank of Ceylon, Annual Reports (various).

[1] All gross domestic fixed capital formation excluding dwellings and buildings.

Foreign Trade

One structural feature which has been referred to earlier concerns the role of foreign trade in the economy of Sri Lanka. We have mentioned the economy's dependence on foreign trade and its role in government resource mobilisation. However, in understanding the structural problems of the estate sector (below) we must also draw attention to trends in export prices of estate crops. Table 2 shows how, rupee, export prices have evolved since 1961 and shows how the barter terms of trade very nearly halved between 1961 and 1977 as export prices lagged far behind import prices. Over the same period the share of tea, rubber and coconuts in total exports fell from 92 to 72 per cent. The volume of estate crop exports rose a little in the late 1960's, only to fall off again in

1977. The purchasing power of estate crop exports over imports was thus
halved during the period. The table also shows the volume of per capita
imports. These clearly fell considerably over the period by 35 per cent.
However, since the mid-1960s the fall is only some 10 per cent. The falling
purchasing power of estate crops is therefore not the predominant determinant
of per capita imports. It can be mentioned also that per capita imports have
remained pretty constantly seven times the corresponding figure for India.

Table 2: Trends in foreign trade

	1961	1965	1970	1975	1977
Export prices, estate crops	100	101	105	178	341
Share of estate crops in total exports (per cent)	92	94	89	76	72
Volume of estate crops	100	117	113	113	100
Barter terms of trade	100	76	57	31	55
Purchasing power of estate crops	100	89	58	32	49
Imports per capita	100	72.5	77.1	67.1	65.4

Source: Central Bank of Ceylon, Annual Reports (various); IMF, International
Monetary Statistics (various).

Structural change in rural areas

Against the background of the pattern of public investment and
changes in foreign trade we can review changes in the rural sector.
Here we look at major trend features leaving a number of major policies
until the next chapter.

We begin this section with a review of data relating to paddy land,
the predominant peasant farming crop. The data in Table 3 give a
broad picture of the evolution of some important factors affecting
the paddy sector. The missing information unfortunately concerns the
current number of parcels per holding. The current total number of
holdings had been estimated at some 800,000 by the Department of
Agrarian Services, this implies some 1.3 parcels per holding and an
average holding size of some 1.5 acres. 1.5 parcels per holding would

give just over 700,000 holdings. In any event the number of parcels per
holding, 1.8 in 1946, must have fallen.

The over-all increase in area since 1946 does not seem large. In
fact, estimates of the area prepared for paddy, especially rain-fed, can
well vary and the above data may minimise the increase. Of the increase
recorded of 283,000 acres the largest parts were in North-central
Province, 100,000 acres, and in Eastern Province, some 80,000 acres.

In three areas, Western, Southern and Sabaragamuwa Provinces, the area
under paddy hardly changed. Parcel sizes fell by considerably more than
the average. Parcels per holding were already lower in those provinces
than elsewhere so the current number of parcels must approximate to the
number of holdings. More paddy operators have been absorbed through the
fragmentation of holdings. Two more provinces, Central and Uva, witnessed
a significant increase in area, but no fall in average parcel size, which
was already low. In those areas, probably more small-holdings of paddy
were created and the average number of parcels per holding reduced. North-
western Province saw both new land coming into cultivation and a fragmentation of parcels. In Northern Province, new land was brought into cultivation but presumably this land was in the less desirable areas south of
Jaffna and the average parcel size increased. Eastern Province had earlier
by far the largest holdings and quite possibly still has. It has in
any event the largest parcels. New land in this Province was often opened
up through major irrigation schemes which would frequently give out paddy
land in only one parcel but of 2-5 acres. North-central Province has, of
course, seen by far the greatest changes. Relatively large holdings with
more parcels per holding than anywhere else have been replaced by a similar
number of larger parcels on better land.

The different experiences of the various provinces exemplify the means
by which more farmers have been absorbed into paddy cultivation. These
can range from new irrigation and colonisation schemes, and squatting
in Eastern and North-central provinces, squatting in Uva, fragmentation
on a diminishing land base in Western Province, fragmentation plus some
expansion in North-western and Central provinces and expansion onto less
favourable land in Northern Province.

Table 3: Sri Lanka, paddy land, 1946-1973

Province	1946				1973		
	Area[1]	Parcels[2]	Average[3]	Parcels/ holding	Area[1]	Parcels[2]	Average[3]
Western	109	99	1.1	1.4	95	146	0.65
Central	77	131	0.6	2.2	92	139	0.65
Southern	136	71	1.9	1.3	137	159	0.9
Northern	99	75	1.3	1.6	130	66	2.0
Eastern	141	22	6.4	3.0	224	60	3.7
North-western	147	137	1.1	1.9	182	230	0.8
North-central	96	126	0.8	4.9	199	114	1.7
Uva	34	45	0.8	1.9	56	69	0.8
Sabaragamuwa	61	66	0.9	1.2	67	109	0.6
Sri Lanka	900	772	1.2	1.8	1183	1092	1.1

Source: Department of Census and Statistics, Survey of Landlessness, 1952, and Census of Agriculture, 1973.

[1] Thousand acres.
[2] Thousands.
[3] Acres.

N.B. A holding can consist of more than one parcel of land.

Of course, this process of fragmentation and a reduction in average paddy holding sizes from some 2.2 acres in 1946 to probably 1.4 or perhaps 1.5 acres today (or a nearly 40 per cent reduction) has in principle probably been compensated by at least a corresponding increase in average yields. However, costs have increased as may have tenancy. As a result real incomes of paddy farmers may well be little different now that at Independence.

The discussion of paddy land revealed considerable differences in holding and parcel sizes between different areas. Unfortunately we have no data to show the size distribution of paddy land alone. The data we have relate to all small-holdings and thus mix in land of different quali- ties, different access to irrigation and supporting different crops. These

Table 4 : Rural Sri Lanka: selected statistics

		1962/63	1971/73	(1946)
I	Rural Employment, thousands	2,597	2,876	
II	Employment in Agriculture, thousands	1,610	1,755	
III	II/I, per cent	62	61	
IV	Cultivators[1] (paddy), thousands	772 (567)	948 (738)	
V	IV/II, per cent	48	54	
VI	Agricultural labourers,[1] thousands	773	713	
VII	VI/II, per cent	48	41	
VIII	Rural Population, 15+, thousands	4,944	5,910	
IX	I/VIII, per cent	52	49	
X	Rural Unemployment, thousands	248	531	
XI	X/VIII, per cent	5	9	
XII	Small-holding area, thousand acres	2,864[2]	3,880[3]	
XIII	Number of Small-holdings, thousands	1,156[2]	1,530[3]	
XIV	XII/XIII, acres	2.47	2.53	(3.31)

Source: Census of Agriculture 1962, 1973. Census of Population 1963, 1971

[1] Rural and estate only.

[2] Excluding areas and holdings of over 25 acres, (see A.T.M. Silva et al. "Sri Lanka country study on rural employment promotion", ILO, Geneva, 1975, Table III-4).

[3] Excluding areas and holdings under one-eighth of an acre.

data suggest that of all holdings under 50 acres in 1973, some 42 per cent of operators (not owners) farmed between one-eighth and one acre, accounting for some 9 per cent of the total area. Just under 3 per cent of operators farmed some 22 per cent of the total. Defective as these data are, they suggest very considerable inequality in the use of farming land.

Against this background we can review some statistics relating to the whole of rural areas, including villages and estates. These are given in Table 4 and rely on the Census of Agriculture and Census of Population undertaken in both the early 1960s and early 1970s.

Unfortunately summary statistics of this type cannot be given for the period before 1962/63. However, developments between 1962/63 and 1971/73 will serve to identify the salient points. One of these is the fall in the share of the employed population from 52 to 49 per cent and the compensating rise in the unemployed population from 5 to 9 per cent. Labour force participation therefore hardly changed. Among the employed the share in agriculture was fairly stationary. Among those employed in agriculture, however, there were major shifts. The absolute numbers of agricultural labourers fell, which strongly suggests that some of them shifted to the "unemployed" category. The absolute number of cultivators (line IV)[1] rose by some 170,000. Very probably this rise was entirely accounted for by the increase in the number of paddy cultivators. The increase in the paddy acreage though was almost certainly minimal so that average paddy holdings fell as we have already noted from some 2.0 to 1.4 acres.

Outside paddy farming the number of full-time cultivators (i.e. cultivators with no paddy, paddy farmers will also have some non-paddy) is less, only around 200,000. Furthermore this figure would not appear to have increased. Some of these cultivators can find a relatively acceptable income from intensive vegetable growing on small plots. The 1971 Census gives 54,000 of these. Others, cultivating low grade tree crops of various kinds, will need at least 5 acre holdings to make a living. Presumably such holdings can no longer be created. Non-paddy farmers with under this acreage will be inevitably part-time farmers. This is the clue to the large disparity between "cultivators" and "holdings". The number of holdings in 1973, in fact, falls not so very far short of the agricultural labour force. However, there is no necessary connection between "part-time farming" (or rather gardening) and labour force status. However, the fact remains that around one-half of the cultivated area in Sri Lanka (excluding holdings of above 20 or 25 acres with plantation crops) is in the hands of part-time cultivators. This is a poor recipe for intensive land use.[2]

---

[1] i.e. those giving "cultivator" as principal occupation.

[2] The Census of Agriculture in fact identified as "part-time" cultivator category, using largely an income definition. Two-thirds of them cultivated under one acre, compared to around one-quarter of "full-time" farmers.

Between 1962 and 1973 the cultivated area recorded by the Agricultural
Census rose by around one million acres and the number of holdings by
nearly 400,000. The marginal holding size was thus very close to the average
so that over the decade average holding sizes remained steady (although
paddy holdings fell in size). The vast bulk of this acreage increase
was in home gardens. Probably these had not been correctly enumerated in
1962, possibly the food shortage of 1973 was forcing an extension of this
kind of, high land, cultivation.

Structural change on estates.

The general impression of the estate sector in Sri Lanka is of a
long period of structural stagnation, broken to an as yet unknowable extent
by land reform in the early 1970s. This stagnation, in over-all acreage,
in holding sizes, in forms of tenure and in labour use and labour relations,
is, however, not so surprising. The estate industry, above all tea and
rubber, has been subject to restriction and control to an extent which
considerably discouraged alterations in its over-all structure since the
1930s. The principal elements were acreage and output restrictions in the
1930s and later exchange control and the Estate Fragmentation Act of 1958.

The principal forms of ownership in this sector have been public and
private companies registered abroad (sterling companies), public and private
companies and unincorporated enterprises of a similar scale in Sri Lanka
(rupee companies and private holdings) and small-holdings. Rupee companies
were as late as the 1930s predominantly owned by non-nationals. However,
it is generally believed (in the absence of complete information) that by
the late 1950s local ownership had almost entirely taken over. Data on
ownership categories after 1958 are perhaps not strictly comparable; they
are as follows:

Table 5: Ownership pattern of tea and rubber areas (thousand acres)

	Tea			Rubber		
	1934	1958	1970	1934	1958	1970
Sterling Coys.	200	202	182	145	91	96
Other estates	335	294	286	336	384	286
Small-holdings (-10 acres)	20	74	103	140	187	185
Total	575	570	571	621	662	567

Source: N. Ramachandran, Foreign Plantation Investment in Ceylon, 1889-1958,
and A.T.M. Silva et al., op. cit. (p. 42).

The data for total rubber acreage vary since some land has definitely been taken out of production. For tea there is next to no variation at all. The 1958 Fragmentation Act did not perhaps totally check the growth of small-holdings in tea although it would appear to have done so for rubber. In tea sterling companies probably made very slight net sales during the 1960s. In rubber they made considerable net sales in the late 1940s and early 1950s.

Sri Lankan authorities, it can be fairly said, have always doubted the capacity of small-holdings to produce estate crops competitively. Thus the Fragmentation Act sets a lower limit of 100 acres to estates. In the 1930s during the period of acreage and output restrictions it would appear that small-holding tea was severely neglected. However, while replanting and other subsidies do also apply to small-holders there is no doubt that, firstly, in the 1930s their sources of finance for land development were meagre (and certainly non-institutional) and secondly that the whole private sector apparatus of support for tea production passed them by. This support apparatus was, in fact, often attacked for being cumbersome and unresponsive to the real needs of the estate industry.[1] In rubber there is a somewhat greater belief that small-holders are competitive. However, efforts at measurement of the real costs involved in the different tenure categories are slight. Small-holders, using their own labour, may well be more profitable. However, both tea and rubber are industrial crops where processing of some kind is part and parcel of production.

In recent years the main attention in the tea and rubber industry has been on two things; relatively high levels of taxation on the one hand, and reinvestment on the other. High levels of taxation, particularly of course export taxation, reduced companies' cash flow and the scope for building up replanting reserves. Foreign capital was still coming into the plantation industry in the early 1950s but by the mid-1950s the likelihood of exchange control and the probability of nationalisation sooner or later had stopped this flow. Replanting, which, agriculturally, was becoming increasingly necessary in the late 1950s and 1960s became the object of a series of subsidies by the government. The results of this were mixed and replanting rates were generally lower than desired. Replanting was also

---

[1] Report of the Commission of Inquiry on Agency Houses and Brokering Firms, S.P. XII, 1974.

carried out with an eye to minimising reductions in cash flow so that, rather than replanting the potentially best areas, companies preferred to replant on the worst. When tea machinery had to be replaced a loan was sought and given by the Asian Development Bank (and passed on to companies - again using the private sector "support apparatus" - at preferential interest rates).

The estate companies responded to what had become an increasingly "uncapitalistic" situation in obvious ways detailed by the Commission of. Inquiry. Sterling companies did everything they could to minimise the effects of exchange control and to keep in being their London operations (for which exchange control exemptions were made). Borrowings within Sri Lanka increased considerably and the Exchange Control authorities permitted sterling companies to take overdrafts to meet all urgent expenses, including Head Office remittances.[1] Rupee companies would appear to have done everything possible to maximise dividends although some companies showed investments either in other plantation companies or in new industries (including tourism). Recent dividends as a percentage of nominal capital issued have been very high; in rupee companies studied by the Commission of Inquiry dividends amounted to 3.5 times issued capital over a 20 year period and to some 95 per cent of post-tax profits. Reserves for replanting were consequently very low. The Commission also noted that rupee companies with substantial outside investments were pre- ferring to take loans for factory development rather than liquidate thise other assets. It was, of course, naive of the Commission of Inquiry to expect either rupee or sterling companies to have spent the 1960s building up reserves to replace their fixed assets. Generally, however, companies appear to have continued necessary maintenance on their estates, including fertilizer use. But, given the absence of a long-term perspective in their planning, the companies have, also predictably, hardly done more to improve the welfare of their labour force than they did before.

---

[1] Report of the Commission of Inquiry, op. cit., p. 247. "The borrowings of the sterling plantation companies from the local banking system have increased with time. The borrowings are such that the aggregate of their liabilities in Sri Lanka almost reaches the realizable value of their assets in Sri Lanka."

Structural change outside agriculture

We have reviewed the changing economic structure of rural Sri Lanka; can anything comparable be proposed for the non-agricultural sectors? Production and operational censuses of the type used for agriculture are not (nor likely to be) available. Industrial censuses or establishment surveys have too narrow a focus for our purpose. One way to begin is through the structure of GDP. Between 1955 and 1975 the share of non-agriculture in GDP[1] rose from 51.6 per cent to 57.8 per cent. However, within this non-agriclutural share there were some major changes, which are given in Table 6. This shows the share of manufacturing doubling over the period and a rise in banking and insurance. Everything else fell, particularly rents (dwellings), public administration and defence and services. These data are not indicative of the share of value added generated in the public sector.

These changes suggest a process of modernisation in which poor quality jobs, e.g. in services, are replaced by more skill-intensive, better-paying and secure employment in manufacturing. In fact, of course one can expect an increase in capital/labour ratios in the more expanding sectors (manufacturing, electricity, perhaps construction) so that the occupational job structure would certainly not change as quickly as the value added structure. As a result one should not be surprised at the continuation of a large amount of unskilled and insecure employment.

Table 7 gives the structure of non-agricultural rural employment and of urban employment in 1963 and 1971. The share of agricultural employment in the total was 52.9 per cent and 50.1 per cent respectively. The time period covered is obviously much shorter than for the GDP analysis, although some of the trends should be common. In 1963 the structure of employment in both rural non-agriculture and in urban areas was very similar. Craft workers, however, particularly in construction, were more numerous in rural areas, clerical and sales workers in urban areas. Personal services were a large share in both. Between 1963 and 1971 there was in both sectors a fall in higher and in clerical occupations, an increase in sales occupations and in certain crafts

---

[1] The 1955 data come from T. Saundranagayam, Central Bank Staff Studies, April 1976. The share of export crop processing in manufacturing is added to "agriculture". It has been taken as 28 per cent of value added in export crop growing.

Table 6: GDP, 1955-1975, current prices (per cent)

	1955	1975
Agriculture[1]	48.4	42.2
Non-agriculture	51.6	57.8
Non-agriculture, of which:		
Manufacturing and mining	11.0	22.4
Construction	8.1	8.0
Electricity	0.3	0.3
Transport and communications	16.6	14.8
Trade	26.9	24.1
Banking and insurance	1.6	2.6
Dwellings	6.1	3.6
Public administration	8.2	6.2
Services	21.3	17.8
Total	100	100

Source: T. Saundranagayam, op. cit.; Central Bank of
Ceylon, Review of the Economy, 1975.

[1] Including processing of export crops.

occupations. Transport and communications rose in rural and fell in
urban areas. Significantly, the share of labour (n.e.c.) rose considerably in both.

Over-all rural non-agricultural employment rose only 16.5 per
cent while urban employment rose 21.8 per cent. Rural unemployment,
as we have seen rose considerably as did urban unemployment (as a
share of the population aged 15+) from 4.6 per cent to 12.9 per cent.

Table 7 : Structure of Employment

	Rural Non-Agriculture		Urban	
	1963	1971	1963	1971
Higher	11.0	9.5	12.0	11.3
Clerical	5.5	5.2	11.5	10.7
Sales - Working Proprietors	7.6	8.0	7.3	8.2
Sales - Other	5.0	5.8	8.4	8.9
Miners	0.5	0.6	-	-
Transport and Communications	6.4	7.4	6.8	6.5
Cloth and Garment Workers	5.7	5.9	2.5	5.7
Construction, Carpentry, etc.	9.9	7.9	6.7	2.8
Food, Beverage, Tobacco	4.3	2.6	1.5	1.1
Other Craft Workers	7.6	10.3	7.0	9.2
(Total Craft Workers)	(27.5)	(26.7)	(17.7)	(18.8)
Protective Services	2.7	2.7	2.9	3.0
Domestic and Hotel Workers	9.0	4.4	13.9	8.7
Barbers, Launderers, etc.	2.7	2.1	1.4	1.3
Other Service Workers	1.1	0.6	0.9	0.7
Labourers n.e.c.	17.5	22.3	13.2	17.2
Occupation unspecified	2.8	5.0	2.2	4.4
TOTAL	100	100	100	100

Source: Department of Census and Statistics, Census of Population, 1963 and 1971

Employment and value-added

In this section we shall summarise a large part of the discussion so far in this chapter. We have seen how some major features have been developing in rural areas, how employment has shifted and where government investment has been located. Here we present a picture for the early 1970s of the over-all breakdown of both employment and of value-added by sector of employment. We refer to pre-land reform days, hence the importance of large-scale private employment in the agricultural sector. Most of this would now fall under the public sector.

Table 8 : Employment and value-added by major employer, early 1970s,
(nos. and Rs.)

	Employment			VA/Employee	
	Public	Private 5+	Private 5-	Public	Private
Non-Agriculture					
Mining and Manufacture	47,300	96,300	166,500	7,657	8,797
Electricity and Water	6,800	200	2,500	6,470	n.a.
Construction	87,200	7,200	18,000	4,805	n.a.
Trade	64,000	23,700	190,600	12,718	10,555
Transport	58,700	2,600	94,000	14,157	10,952
Financial Services	14,000	1,500	10,900	16,428	8,548
Other Services	341,300	22,300	191,700	4,946	⎰
Not Adequately Defined[1]	-	-	106,600	-	⎱ 4,345
Total Non-Agriculture	669,200	153,600	780,800	7,119	8,293
Agriculture (specified)	126,400	382,200	1,315,300	-	-
Not Adequately Defined[2]	-	-	191,700		
Total Agriculture	126,400	382,200	1,507,000	12,547	3,980
Total Sri Lanka	795,600	535,800	2,287,800	7,981	5,408

Source: Central Bank of Ceylon, Annual Report 1975, Department of Census
and Statistics, Census of Population 1971; Department of Labour,
Employment Survey 1975; P.M. Radhakrishnan, Ministry of
Planning, op. cit.

[1] Urban.

[2] Rural.

Table 8 rests on a number of sources. It uses the Employment
Survey data of 1975 and also some employment data given by the Central
Bank for 1975. The data for establishments with under 5 employees are
calculated as a residual using the employment data of the Census in 1971.

Any over-all employment growth between 1971 and 1975 should be added
to the figures for that column. Public "other services" is calculated
by adding to the data from the Employment Survey the total given for
employment in government departments by the Central Bank report minus the
total of employment in government departments included in the employment
survey.[1]

The value-added breakdown relies considerably on the data produced by
Radhakrishnan which separate the public sector share from the rest. In
addition the value-added in processing tea and rubber has been shifted from
manufacturing to agriculture. It goes without saying that none of the
data given are to be taken as more than an indicator of orders of magnitude.

The data present many points of interest. Within non-agricultural
employment the public sector accounts for over 40 per cent and the "larger
scale" (over five employees) private sector for under 10 per cent.
Employment in more traditional government activities accounts for only
around one-half of non-agricultural public sector employment with very
large shares also reported for manufacturing and construction. Manufacturing includes a considerable number of low productivity activities,
including weaving centres. As a result value-added per public sector
manufacturing worker is relatively low. This contrasts with the
obviously high levels of value-added per worker in many capital-
intensive government corporations. Thus government manufacturing
activities are not predominantly in the modern, large-scale sector.
However, the converse is very probably true.

Manufacturing is the predominant activity of the larger-scale
private sector (outside agriculture). Construction, for example, is
either in the public sector or in the small-scale sector, but hardly in-
between. Trade is another case in point. The small-scale sector, on
the other hand, has three major points of concentration; manufacturing,
trade and other services, followed by transport. These are the
areas where one can expect the greatest amount of unorganised labour

---

[1] These were the Buildings, Co-operative development, Marketing,
Public trustees and Small industries departments. Their total of employment was 91,450 of which the second and last contributed some 77,000.

and the "informal sector" to be prevalent.

The low level of value-added per employee in public sector manufacturing has already been mentioned. In other sectors public sector employment has generally a high value-added per worker although for "other services" the difference would not appear very great. There is a very great difference in the data for agriculture. In fact, putting all "inadequately defined" in rural areas into agriculture inevitably lowers the private sector share to an exaggerated extent. Furthermore, if it is assumed that the 5+ workers have the same level of value-added in agriculture as public sector workers, then the corresponding figure for the small-scale sector falls to Rs. 1,800.

Land reform

In the preceding sections we have seen some major but usually gradual developments. Government has invested continually in manufacturing and in new land development. The latter, however, has not been sufficient to stop paddy holding sizes from falling. The estate sector stagnated and rural unemployment increased. In urban areas the fast growth of manufacturing output was unable to prevent increasing segmentation in the labour market. The land reform exercise, which took place in two parts in 1972 and 1975, can be seen against this background. It represents probably the most far-reaching attempt by any government to change the economic structure of the country. The two different parts of land reform corresponded fairly closely to the distinction between larger smallholdings and smaller estates on the one hand, and major estates on the other. As such the background to the two rounds of take-over was different. Indeed it had been argued in the Seers report[1] that while major estates might be left untouched, the first round of the reform should have imposed lower ceilings than it later did.

---

[1] Matching employment opportunities and expectations: a programme of action for Ceylon, ILO Geneva, 1971.

The 1971 insurgency lent a particular urgency to the 1972 Land
Reform Law although this must be seen against a background of strong
feeling for the Kandyan peasant and a general belief that very many smaller
estates were inefficiently managed. However, the 1975 take-over of
public company lands in addition owed something both to the UK campaign
drawing attention to the living standards of estate workers and to a sale
of some 30,000 acres to Kuwaiti interests. It was also hoped that
"voluntary" repatriation of Indian workers would be speeded up by the
take-over. However, much of the interest of the land reform comes
in the way it was managed, the way the lands were later administered and the
opportunities thus opened.

The first round of land reform provided for the appropriation, with
compensation, of owned holdings of over 25 acres of paddy or 50 acres
of other land from private owners and, in the second round, of total
appropriation of land owned by public companies. Parents of owners and
also children over 18 could also hold land up to the ceiling but such
intra-family transfers were permitted only at the discretion of the
land reform commissions. This distinction between land belonging to individuals and private companies under the 1972 law and to public companies
(from which a little under half the appropriated land was foreign owned)
under the 1975 law was a legal distinction. Certainly, these public
companies averaged over 1,000 acres of cultivated land each but the 1972
Census of Agriculture records an additional 351 non-public companies
operating over 500 acres each.[1] Thus, even in round I some very
large holdings were taken over, with the authorities a great deal less
prepared for their management than they were to be in 1975. The
State Plantations Corporation took some 33,000 acres of these larger
estates but, by 1976, a new organisation, the Usawasama (Upcountry
Co-operative Estates Development Board) was managing some 65,000 acres.
It was wound up in 1977.

---

[1] Assuming that all operated holdings of public companies fell
into the 500 acre and above category.

From the basic needs viewpoint such a land reform can have
three possible types of benefits: it can quickly redistribute income
streams from one set of owners to another set of owner (cultivators):[1]
after some while it can create more employment through better management of the capital stock and, finally, it can redistribute political
influence in line with the redistributed assets. So far some, but, most
probably very slight, benefits under the first two headings have probably
accrued. However, they may well have been offset by the disruption and
frequent mismanagement which elsewhere often led to a fall in e.g. employment levels. The creation of benefits under the third heading was most
strongly opposed by those with most to lose, namely existing political
representatives.

Under the first round of land reform some 383,000 acres of cultivated
land were appropriated. Only 18,000 were in paddy, the rest were plantation
crops. This analysis will therefore proceed in terms of plantation crops.
An additional 176,000 acres of uncultivated lands were also taken over, a
matter to which we shall revert. In order to identify the holding sizes
from which these lands were taken we shall start from the hypothesis that
lands in the holding size class of 50-100 acres were generally untouched.
In the holding size class of 100 acres + (excluding public companies) were,
in 1962, 2,575 operated holdings with some 550,000 acres. 356,000 acres
were appropriated, leaving on average 72 acres per holding. A post land
reform average size of 70 acres seems feasible. It suggests, of course,
that some holdings in the 50-100 acre class were affected. However, even
if 20 per cent of holdings in that size class lost 20 acres each their total
loss would be only 10,000 acres. It seems reasonable to suggest that the
average post land reform size of affected holdings was nearer 70 than 80
acres. Thus, taking the traditional definition of "estates" as above 50
acres, it appears that 70 per cent of estate land was taken over in both
rounds, reducing private holdings in that category from 1,122,800 acres to
331,000 acres. Slightly under one half was taken in round I, slightly more
in round II. Taking both rounds together the share of acreage under different crops which was taken over was as follows, in per cent:

	Tea	Rubber	Coconut and other
As share total area of Sri Lanka	66	31	20
As share estates 100 acres and above	88	55	100

---

[1] Apparently, "reasonable" compensation is being paid and now (1979)
in a period of import liberalisation, is being spent on imported goods
financed by foreign loans.

The definition of the land ceiling used in round I guaranteed that
a very large array of disparate parcels of varying size and with various
standing crops would be appropriated. Acquisitions could range from one
acre of unused semi-jungle land to 1,000 acres of well managed tea land.
A wide range of administrative and institutional responses were thus called
for. In addition an owned holding could well consist of a number of parcels;
the land reform authorities could thus find themselves in possession of
small extents of land several miles apart. In this respect clearly experience varied between districts, as shown in Table 9. In Colombo district
some 7,600 parcels averaging 3 acres were taken over; in Nuwara Eliya only
79 parcels averaging 364 acres. Thus the institutional response to land
reform depended at least on 1) the amount of cultivable land taken over in
any locality and 2) the average parcel size.

But, in fact, there was a third and, in certain respects, compelling
constraint. On average nearly one-fifth of an acre per head of the agricultural population was taken. In Puttalam, for example, appropriated land
amounted to one-half an acre per person engaged in agriculture. Thus it
might appear that the prospects for spreading land among the agricultural
population were good. But the cultivated land taken over was nearly all,
although to very varying degrees, carrying a permanent or casual work force,
the degree varying obviously between the major crops. The scope for redistribution to outsiders was that much reduced unless the existing labour was
to be displaced. That many of the permanent labourers were non-citizens
only complicated the issues. Forms of co-operative management involving the
existing labour force and avoiding the disruption of normal production were
therefore attractive propositions for land taken over in manageable units,
particularly for coconut lands with good potential for diversification.

Between districts average parcel size varied considerably. So did
other factors. Taking again the category 100 acres and above (excluding
public companies) Table 9 also shows the changes in average size before
and after round I. Clearly considerable variation remained with holdings
in Galle and Badulla up to 190 acres and the rest varying between some 70-130
acres. This may represent a discriminating application of the provisions of
the law on intra-family transfers.[1] In addition the amount of jungle and
uncultivated land acquired shows extreme variation. For Badulla and

---

[1] However, while these provisions were not applied uniformly there
seems no reason to expect a systematic bias by district.

Ratnapura more such land was taken over than was declared in the 1962
Census of Agriculture for all holding size groups. But in a number of
districts the extent of jungle and uncultivated land taken over was far in
excess of any figure the 1962 census might suggest for the relevant holding
size group.

Turning to the institutional forms which accounted for the acquired
land, Table 9 gives details. The table includes electoral land reform co-
operatives (aboloshed in 1977), Janawasas (youth co-operative projects) and
individual land alienation. Excluded are Usawasamas[1] (as district level
data for them are not available) and a number of less important institutional
forms. Usawasamas were clearly most important in the up-country estate
areas.

The amount of land distributed to villagers, and the amount planned
for land redistribution, varied considerably between districts. In Kandy
some 20,000 acres were scheduled for redistribution, in Galle 2,200 acres.
In fact Kandy, Kurunegala, Puttalam, Moneragala, Amparai and Jaffna seem
to have distributed land most speedily. However, there must be a suspicion, at least for Moneregala, that the land distributed was previously
uncultivated and thus required considerable development. The slowest rate
of redistribution seems to have come precisely in those over-populated areas
where the reverse could have been expected, i.e. Colombo, Kalutara, Galle,
Matara and Kegalle. In these areas a very large number of very small parcels were acquired; their speedy redistribution would have seemed desirable.

It has interestingly been pointed out that most of the paddy lands
taken over could not be split up and given to the landless.[2] Most of
these lands were tenanted and, under the Paddy Lands Act, large holdings
cultivated by tenants using hired labour were inviolate. Ownership, therefore, passed to the Land Reform Commission. But the redistribution programme has come under other forms of criticism. Sometimes only very small
amounts of land, perhaps one-quarter of an acre, were distributed and even
then these lands might well be some distance from the recipients' village.
No facilities to develop the land were provided and, above all, no secure
titles were given. As a result it would appear, especially around tea

---

[1] Up-country Co-operative Estate Development Board.

[2] See Agrarian Research and Training Institute, "Agrarian Reform and
Rural Development in Sri Lanka", Colombo, 1978.

Table 9: Land reform, round I, district averages[1]

	Land at risk: thousand acres (I)	Taken over: thousand acres (II)	Average holding size before round I: acres (III)	Average holding size after round I: acres (IV)	Paddy land acquired: thousand acres (V)	Jungle recorded in 1962 Census: thousand acres (VI)	Jungle land acquired: thousand acres (VII)	Janawasas thousand acres (VIII)	ELRCs thousand acres (IX)	Land distributed thousand acres (X)	Scheduled for distribution: thousand acres (XI)	Parcel size: acres (XII)
Kandy	98.9	68.5	327	100	-	18.0	14.4	2.2	28.2	13.7	6.3	66
Matale	29.7	24.7	294	49	1.2	10.3	10.1	1.3	-	3.4	4.5	130
Nuwara Eliya	28.4	18.4	383	134	-	0.9	10.3	-	-	0.2	5.3	364
Badulla	29.3	13.1	337	188	-	2.7	31.8	0.8	15.9	0.5	10.6	129
Ratnapura	58.5	29.6	216	107	2.5	5.0	42.9	1.9	16.3	2.3	6.6	44
Kegalle	56.4	34.4	303	118	-	3.7	9.4	1.5	33.7	0.2	7.7	63
Colombo	50.7	20.0	178	108	1.2	2.8	1.1	-	10.3	0.7	5.7	3
Kalutara	44.8	27.3	297	116	1.1	0.9	1.8	4.8	16.2	0.3	3.4	71
Galle	33.8	13.0	307	190	0.6	2.2	8.4	11.1	3.6	0.4	1.8	41
Matara	27.9	15.6	249	110	1.2	8.1	8.3	5.4	8.2	0.3	2.6	28
Kurunegala	100.6	59.4	190	78	2.3	12.7	2.6	11.9	15.7	8.9	3.2	71
Puttalam	46.4	26.4	180	77	1.5	10.5	16.2	3.4	25.0	7.8	0.9	55
Hambantota	2.4	1.6	74	23	1.6	4.9	3.1	0.3	1.0	1.0	1.4	27
Moneregala	8.9	7.2	554	105	0.1	4.4	10.4	0.3	4.3	6.7	-	9
Jaffna	7.6	3.2	120	70	0.6	4.2	1.1	0.5	-	3.4	-	26
Batticaloa	4.7	3.2	131	43	1.5	3.8	-	-	-	0.4	2.7	15
Amparai	3.1	1.2	155	98	1.2	3.1	0.4	-	-	1.6	-	23
Sri Lanka	544.6	364.0	211	70	18.4	101.4	176.5	49.9	178.4	52.2	69.6	23

1 Excluding Mannar, Vavuniya, Trincomalee, Anuradhapura and Pollonaruwa.

Source: Department of Census and Statistics, Census of Agriculture, 1962, and data supplied by the Land Reform Committee.

(See next page for explanation of titles)

Table 9: explanation of titles

I: <u>Land at risk</u> - total of plantation crops from estates 100 acres and above minus plantation crops taken over in round II; thousand acres.

II: <u>Taken over</u> - plantation crops only; thousand acres.

III: <u>Average holding size before round I</u> - holdings over 100 acres excluding public companies; acres.

IV: <u>Average holding size after round I</u> - holdings over 100 acres excluding public companies; acres.

V: <u>Paddy land acquired</u> - thousand acres.

VI: <u>Jungle recorded in 1962 Census</u> - jungle and uncultivated lands recorded as part of 100 acres and over holdings in 1962 minus "other" category in public company land acquired; thousand acres.

VII: <u>Jungle land acquired</u> - thousand acres.

VIII: <u>Janawasas</u> - area of Janawasas at end 1976; thousand acres.

IX: <u>ELRCs</u> - Area of Electoral Land Reform Co-operatives at end 1975; thousand acres.

X: <u>Land distributed</u> - area of land distributed to villagers,.mid-1976; thousand acres.

XI: <u>Scheduled for distribution</u> - area of land to be distributed to villagers, end 1976; thousand acres.

XII: <u>Parcel size</u> - average size of parcel of all types of land acquired; acres.

estates, that some land given out to individuals reverted to government owned estates in 1977.

The other major institutional forms were the Janawasas, which continue to exist as co-operatives, and the Electoral Land Reform Co-operatives (ELRC). The latter, which had the local Member of Parliament (or rather National State Assembly) as Chairman, took over the bulk of the land managed at first by the District Land Reform Authorities thus representing the increasing role of party-political influence in land reform implementation. Janawasas clearly co-existed with ELRCs in most districts although,

strangely, they predominated in Galle. In certain up-country districts
there were apparently no ELRCs leaving local politicians to exercise
their influence through appointments and management of the Usawasamas.
Further discussion on the working of these institutions we leave to
Chapter 7 on Administration and Participation.

The second round of land reform calls for very little comment.
By 1975 an additional government estate management corporation, the
Janawasama, was set up and the acquired estates were divided between it
and the State Plantation Corporation. Existing management was generally
retained and little or no change in day-to-day running of the estates
was introduced. This was indicative of an increased concern with the maintenance of output levels and with re-investment. Nevertheless there were
certain attempts by local politicians to redistribute land individually
in a hasty and unplanned manner. Indeed, the transparently partisan
nature of these attempts probably made them the easier to reverse in 1977.

Criticisms of the handling of the lands acquired under land reform
must remember three major constraints, the considerable variation in parcel
size and cropping pattern, the existence of permanent labour on larger
holdings and, no doubt, the poor quality of much of the land taken over.
The smoothness and order of the transition from private to public ownership may reflect the private owners' ability to "make the best of a bad
job" and dispose of their worst lands. Thus raising productivity levels
on precisely those lands was going to be difficult. Nevertheless an
expanded and better handled programme of land redistribution to the
landless and to marginal farmers would have helped to solve some of the
problems of inconveniently small units. Clearly, in many Janawasas
especially, serious attempts were made to upgrade lands and diversify
crops, particularly under coconut, as the experts had long recommended.
Such steps were, and are, necessary under any management system. On many
other lands it would appear that there was more mismanagement than
management.

But the major comment on land reform is that despite its extent
the rural social and economic structure was hardly changed. Firstly
the ceiling, which was probably effectively some 70 acres on average,
left the larger village-based landlords untouched. Popular participation
was discouraged in favour of indirect participation through, and direct
control by, political representatives. Largely as a result of these facts

estates and villages were no more integrated afterwards than before.
Village groups had no say in disposing of estate land and seem to have never
gone beyond the stage of preparing lists of landless families, lists which
were generally disregarded. Sometimes, indeed, estate-village relations
worsened when easy-going ways of former owners allowing the grazing of
village cattle were replaced by more determined management. One might
indeed say that the state was insufficiently prepared for land reform
and for the inevitable demands which would be made by local politicians
on the government side.

PART IV: Selected Policies

CHAPTER 6
Rural Policies

Introduction

In this chapter we turn our attention to the income distribution
and welfare effects of a number of major policies affecting the rural
sector. Unlike land reform, where a once and for all change in ownership
was secured, these policies have operated over a long period of time
and their effects have been at work more insidiously. We discuss four
issues here, the regulation of tenancy and the effectiveness of the Paddy
Lands Act, the guaranteed price scheme for paddy, input supply programmes
and resettlement (colonisation and major irrigation) programmes. Some
of these programmes have no doubt been effective in raising output in the
aggregate but have had clearly undesirable welfare effects. Conversely
action on the regulation of tenancy has probably achieved neither welfare
nor output objectives and may indeed have had perverse effects on both
counts.

Regulation of tenancy and share cropping

Tenancy in Sri Lanka ("Ande") is mostly confined to the paddy sector.
It affects almost 25-30 per cent of paddy lands and constitutes the most
significant tenure problem given its association with high rents and
insecurity. The first serious attempt to regulate tenancy was made with
the Paddy Lands Act of 1958 which was intended to ensure greater security
and reduced rents. These provisions have been in operation for almost
20 years and it is widely accepted that they have by and large failed
to improve the position of tenants.

Data from the Census of Agriculture in 1946 and in 1962 show that
the proportion of land under tenancy has remained more or less constant
at some 25 to 30 per cent of total paddy land.[1] The acreage under share
cropping is highest (40 per cent or more) in the South (Hambantota and
Matara) and Central Highland regions of the country, while in the Western
and South-West lowlands the proportion is closer to the island's average.
In the remaining parts of the country (mainly Dry Zone areas) tenancy is
not widespread, the proportion of land under Ande being less than 20 per

---

[1] A report on paddy statistics gave 29 per cent as the extent of land
cultivated by share croppers in 1954/55.

cent. Tenancy could therefore be considered as a serious problem mainly in the Central, South and possibly South-West regions where pressure of population on land is acute. In Hambantota large tracts of absentee owned paddy lands are cultivated by tenants through local agents called Gambaraya. In the East Coast areas, where paddy cultivation is commercialised, large holdings are operated by intermediaries using hired labour. The labourers are sometimes paid in kind and the system is a kind of share cropping.[1]

Recent official figures on the total number of tenants and owner-tenants are given in Table 1.

Table 1: Tenure of paddy lands

Type of tenure	Operators	
	Number	Per cent
Ande cultivators	368,511	28.2
Owner cultivators	840,838	64.4
Owner cum-Ande	82,994	6.4
Landowners using only hired labour	13,021	1.1
TOTAL	1,305,364	100.0

Source: Ministry of Agriculture and Lands, Colombo, 1977

The data no doubt relate to registered tenants but large numbers generally remain unregistered.[2] Information available from sample surveys for several districts reveal that the numbers are certainly larger (Table 2).

Before the Paddy Lands Act the Ande tenant was only a share cropper at will. He had no legal claim to the land and could be evicted at any time without compensation. Evictions were reported to have been common before

[1] Under the Nalukooddu arrangement the Veliyan performs similar functions to those of a share tenant in Sinhalese areas. But the Veliyan according to traditional customs is treated as a paid cultivator and he is paid a fixed share. The lands he cultivates are entered in the register in the landlord's name and the landlord is considered the rightful owner cultivator. The Nalukoodu system is clearly a system of concealed tenancy. See A. Hameed et al. Rice Revolution in Sri Lanka, UNRISD, 1977.

[2] A recent village study found that only 17-23 per cent of the tenants were registered. See A. Hameed, op. cit., p. 204.

1958. In the overcrowded areas many evictions resulted from the landlords offering tenancies to the highest bidders, almost every season.

Table 2: Tenure of paddy lands (selected districts)

	Per cent of operators				Total no. of operators in sample
	Owner	Tenant	Owner-tenant	Other[1]	
Kandy	38	40	22	-	158
Kegalle	49	40	11	-	164
Colombo	51	39	10	-	143
Hambantota	21	49	24	6	156

Source:Agrarian Researchand Training Institute (ARTI), The Agrarian Situation Relating to Paddy Cultivation in Five Selected Districts of
Sri Lanka, Colombo 1975.
[1] Mainly encroachers.

Pre-1958 rents appear to have varied between one-quarter to one-half
of the produce, although the 50 per cent crop share had generally been the
most widespread arrangement. However, in some areas rents were as high
as two-thirds of total produce. Resident landlords usually charged 50
per cent of the produce and most of them provided the tenant with essential
inputs such as seed paddy and fertilizer to be recovered after harvest
with interest paid at high rates of up to 100 per cent.[1] Twenty-five
per cent of the crop share was paid to absentee landlords who offered no
assistance to the tenants. This system was prevalent mostly in the
Hambantota and East Coast areas where the land was managed by an intermediary. In Hambantota, the tenants were obliged to obtain from the intermediary (Gambaraya) all the seed, fertilizer, tractors, sprayers and credit,
for which exhorbitant interest rates were charged in addition to a part
of the produce. The "Veliyan" under the Nalukooddu system in the East
Coast generally retained around 15 per cent of the produce.

For most tenants, their dependence on the landlords went beyond land
and inputs. Many landless tenants lived on lands belonging to the landlord.
In other cases, the tenant and his family members depended on the landlord
for work on his other lands such as coconut or rubber. In many areas, the

---

[1] W.M. Tilakaratne, Agricultural Credit in a Developing Economy,
Central Bank of Ceylon, Colombo, 1962.

tenants had to perform services such as transporting the landlord's crop share to his home, attending to various cultivation operations on the landlord's plots free of charge and assisting him in household work connected with festivals and ceremonies. In addition, token cash gifts (madaran) had to be given to landlords at the beginning of each cultivation season as a symbol of loyalty in order to be assured of continued cultivation rights.

The Paddy Lands Act No. 1 of 1958 was the first serious legislative attempt[1] taken to regulate share tenancy. Its main objectives were:

1. To confer permanent and heritable tenancy rights on share croppers. The tenants were empowered to name their successors. Evictions were thus made an illegal and a punishable offence. Landlords were given the concession of resuming cultivation on a maximum extent of 5 acres after meeting valid claims for compensation by the tenants affected.

2. To restrict rents to a maximum of 25 per cent of produce or 12 bushels per acre, whichever is less or a minimum of 2 bushels per acre or one-eighth of yield whichever is less, the variation being related to yield differences in different areas.

3. To regulate interest rates and hire charges for implements and draft animals provided by landlords to tenants.

4. To organise Cultivation Committees which would (a) act as village level instruments for implementing the reforms and (b) undertake the organisation and development of paddy cultivation.

Implementation was placed in the hands of a new Department of Agrarian Services under the Ministry of Food and Agriculture. Assistant Commissioners (one for each district) were given the powers to inquire into and decide on tenancy disputes. A Board of Review was provided to hear appeals against decisions of these Assistant Commissioners. The Paddy Lands Act was replaced by the Agricultural Lands Law of 1973, incorporating all the provisions on tenancy. Under the agricultural productivity

---

[1] An initial attempt to regulate tenancy was made with the introduction of the Paddy Lands Act of 1953 which made provision for granting tenure security for 5 years, for registration of tenancy agreements and for maximum rents. This act was applied only in two districts and that not effectively. Hence, it was not a serious attempt to remedy Ande tenancy although it evoked interest in the problem and the need for reforming it.

law of 1972, agricultural tribunals were established to replace the
national Board of Review which had failed to settle the multitude of tenancy
cases adequately and speedily. Decisions of the agricultural tribunals
were final and could not be questioned in any court of law. However,
these tribunals came into operation only in 1975 and were disbanded in mid-
1977.

At the village level the Cultivation Committees (one for 200-400 acres
of paddy land) were expected to be the main instruments for implementing
tenancy provisions.[1] Each committee was originally to consist of 12 members, elected by the farmers. But the members of the Cultivation
Committees set up under the Agricultural Lands Law and the members of the
Agricultural Productivity Committees (10 for each) were appointed by the
Minister of Agriculture on the recommendation of the area politician.

The introduction of the Paddy Lands Act was immediately followed by
a spate of evictions throughout the country. At the end of its first year
of operation, 14,500 evictions were reported which by 1960 had increased
to 18,000.[2] Between 1958 and 1972 a total of 43,134 complaints of evictions were received. Less than 25 per cent of these resulted in the resto-
ration of the rights of the evicted tenants through legal or conciliatory
procedures. By 1971 there were still a large number of complaints
awaiting inquiry, some as far back as 1958.[3]

Reported data on evictions say very little about the total number of
evictions. Many tenants, through fear of retaliatory action by the landlords, may not have reported their evictions or may have voluntarily

---

[1] In addition to their general development functions affecting the
paddy sector the Cultivation Committees were empowered to (a) maintain
a Cultivators' Register giving details such as tenure, size and location
of paddy lands; (b) look into disputes among cultivators or between owners
and tenants; and (c) appoint a tenant where a tenant had died or renounced
his tenancy without nominating the successor.

[2] Until 1963, the Act was operational only in two disticts. The
delay in making it fully operational simultaneously over the entire Island
was mainly responsible for this initial wave of evictions. Until 1963
tenants in the districts outside the two which came under the ministerial
decree were unable to take legal action against evictions.

[3] I.K. Weerawardana, Lessons of an Experiment, the Paddy Lands Act of
1958, Ministry of Agriculture and Lands, Colombo, 1975.

surrendered their tenancy rights or have even accepted a derogation of their
status to agricultural labourers as a means of survival. Several evaluation studies conducted since 1958 have come to the general conclusion
that the provisions relating to tenancy security have failed to achieve
their objectives.[1] Most of these studies have shown that almost 50 per
cent of tenants did not attempt to register themselves in the Paddy Lands
Register through fear of eviction and a similar proportion continued to
pay the half share of produce for the same reason. Thus the problem of
insecurity remains basically unaltered. Growing unemployment may have
made it worse in recent years. Similarly, controlled rents cannot be
achieved without security of tenure.

An all-island survey of the Cultivation Committees undertaken by the
Department of Agrarian Services in 1966 showed that in the Eastern,
South-Eastern and North-Eastern parts of the island the landowners'
share of the crop averaged 25 per cent or less.[2] In these areas the
paddy fields were developed in the recent past and strong customs
governing rents were absent. Labour had been in short supply and competition for land was less acute than in the Wet Zone areas. However, "in
the absence of any specific information on rents in the pre-reform period
any conclusion drawn about the impact of the reform on rents from data on
post reform rent levels has to remain conjectural".[3] Nevertheless, the
majority of tenants are in no position to pay whichever is less of the two
rents stipulated in the Act.

In most upcountry areas and some Wet Zone low country areas such as
Kurunegala and Colombo, a majority of the tenants still continue to pay

---

[1] A.B. Jayasinghe,"Survey of Cultivation Committees", Department
of Agrarian Services, Colombo, 1966; Ameer Raza, Evaluation of the
Paddy Lands Act, FAO, Rome, 1967; and R.D. Wanigaratne, W. Gooneratne
and N. Shanmugaratnam, Policies and Implementation of Land Reform in Sri
Lanka - Case Studies, ARTI, Colombo, 1978.

[2] Department of Agrarian Services, op. cit.

[3] G.H. Peiris, "Share tenancy and tenurial reform in Sri Lanka",
Ceylon Journal of Historical and Social Studies, New Series, Vol. 5(1),
1976.

over and above the rents stipulated by the Act.[1] These are the most
densely populated areas in the country where landlessness is acute and
alternative job opportunities absent. Tenants have very little bargaining
power. Even in most Dry Zone areas where landlessness is not a serious
problem rents paid averaged half of produce.[2] As most landlords receiving
a half share of produce also provided certain inputs at high interest rates
the tenants in fact retained much less than 50 per cent of the total production. Table 3 gives some idea of rent payments in the early 1970s for
several districts.

Table 3: Rent payment in selected districts, per cent of tenants paying

	Fixed rent	25 per cent share	Whichever is less	50 per cent	Others
Hambantota	12	69	3	3	13
Kandy	11	5	-	83	1
Kegalle	8	1	-	85	7
Colombo	4	14	-	74	8

Source: ARTI, The Agrarian Situation ..., op. cit.

The provisions relating to the regulation of interest rates on inputs
provided by landlords to tenants remained almost a dead letter in the face
of frustrated attempts at implementing the security of tenure and rent
provisions.

The failure of the Paddy Lands Act to make a significant break-
through in improving tenancy relations has a variety of interrelated
reasons. The major blow to its effective implementation was the weakness
of the legislation itself. It had to be amended five times between 1958
and 1970 in order to prevent the eviction of tenants and to make
the Cultivation Committees more effective in promoting the objectives of

---

[1] ARTI, The Agrarian Situation ..., op. cit.

[2] Hameed et al., op. cit.

the Act.[1] Successive amendments only demonstrated the weakness of the law. By taking advantage of these weaknesses landlords were always able to prevent the tenants from assuming their rights in several ways. These included the:

(a) registration of the landlord as the actual cultivator of the Ande land;

(b) registration of the tenant as an agricultural labourer; or

(c) the rotation of the land among several tenants thus preventing them from claiming continuity of tenancy.

The landlords have thus been able to prevent the registration of the tenants in the Paddy Lands Register maintained by the Cultivation Committee, which serves as the only legal proof of tenancy.

All this has led to a feeling of doubt in the minds of the tenants regarding the ability of the law to grant them full protection. No landlord has been prosecuted during the entire period for charging rents above the stipulated level. In any event few tenants are able to take even the slightest risk of eviction by attempting to pay the stipulated rent. A tenant evicted for attempting to register himself in the Paddy Lands register or for trying to pay the stipulated rent, and who failed to get himself reinstated was branded as a trouble-maker and rarely obtained a piece of land from any other landowner in the village.

The disbandment of the Agricultural Productivity Committees and Cultivation Committees in mid-1977 has brought about a situation where the tenancy provisions are simply held in abeyance. Agricultural tribunals are not functioning, which means evicted tenants have no way of complaining. In this situation evictions no doubt have increased.

---

[1] The Act (especially the authority of Assistant Commissioners to adjudicate complaints of evictions) was challenged in the Law Courts on several occasions until it was finally settled in 1970 when the Supreme Court decided in favour of the Assistant Commissioners' authority to decide on eviction cases. Most evicted tenants, however, had to wait for redress until the setting up of the agricultural tribunals under the Agricultural Productivity Law of 1972 and these tribunals were finally set up only in 1975 but were disbanded in mid-1977. In addition, the Cultivation Committees which were expected to implement the provisions of the Act at the village level ran into several legal problems from the very beginning. These included questioning the legality of the Committees that have not been fully constituted as specified by the Act (three non-cultivating owners were required to be members of the Committees, but in order to sabotage they avoided participation, this requirement was removed in 1964) and their virtual non-recognition by other governmental agencies.

The Cultivation Committees were expected to implement tenancy provisions at the village level and to look after the interest of the tenant
population. However, these committees commenced and continued as weak institutions where their legality was questioned and authority not recognised by
other governmental agencies. Economically, they never commanded adequate
financial and other resources to function effectively. Despite several
efforts to amend the law these basic weaknesses continued even in the later
years,[1] almost until their reorganisation in 1973 under the Agricultural
Lands Law.

But the Cultivation Committees never became representative of the underprivileged, particularly tenants, although they were intended to create
a strong farmer organisation at village level. Many studies[2] have shown
that from their inception these Committees were dominated by the traditional
village leadership, landowners, businessmen and professional classes, who
wielded influence with the area politician and the officialdom. As a
result the Committees were not committed to safeguard the interests of
the tenants and the tenants themselves had very little faith in the Committees. Most Committees were unable to muster the support of the general
body of cultivators,[3] and were neither favourably disposed to nor interested
in assisting tenants to organise themselves.

Had the Cultivation Committees been properly constituted by eliminating
vested interests[4] and had the implementing department played a more active
role in promoting tenant solidarity and participation in committee affairs,

---

[1] In the mid-1960s almost 70 per cent of the Committees collected
less than 50 per cent of the acreage levy (their main source of finance)
and the same proportion of Committees had no offices of their own or paid
officials for their administrative work.

[2] G.H. Peiris, op. cit. gives a large number of references on this
issue. Hameed et al. op. cit. and R.D. Wanigaratne, W. Gooneratne and
N. Shanmugaratnum, op. cit. give further evidence to support this.

[3] G.H. Peiris, op. cit.

[4] This was expected of the reorganisation of Cultivation Committees
under the Agricultural Lands Law of 1973. However under the nominative
principle it was again the elitist groups with vested interests who were
appointed to the Committees. There was little or no improvement in tenant
representation.

the implementation process might have taken a somewhat different
direction. But the tenant cultivators were unable to organise themselves without some form of external assistance. Thus the Ande cultivators'
associations which sprang up with the introduction of the Paddy Lands Act
in areas where insecurity of tenancy had been a regular feature[1] failed
to survive long. Even in Hambantota where large extents of absentee owned
paddy tracts were cultivated by tenants under the Gambararaya system organised action by the tenants was lacking.

The tenants' position has probably worsened by the combined impact
of increasing rural unemployment and the spread of new technology. The
acuteness of the unemployment problem in rural areas has increased competition for tenancy rights even to small plots as, no doubt, has the spread
of new rice technology and potentially greater profits in paddy cultivation.

There is, however, little evidence of eviction of tenants by larger
owners to resume own cultivation by mechanising operations. Mechanisation
in Sri Lanka has progressed rather slowly and tractors, mostly in the Dry
Zone, have replaced animal power and not labour. But unemployment in rural
areas is transforming tenancy into a form of cheap labour supply. Tenancy
is more advantageous to the landlord than cultivating the land himself using
wage labour. It not only assures a steady supply of labour (it is in
fact labour attached to land) but enables the transfer of a part of the loss
from crop failure to the tenant.

Thus the failure of tenancy reforms amidst increasing landlessness and
unemployment and the rapid spread of new technology seems to have brought
about a situation where "tenancy" is preferred to personal cultivation,
tenancy is preferred to wage labour but hired labour preferred to mechanisation.

Guaranteed prices and produce collection

During the Second World War with the interruption of food imports
from abroad the Colonial Government imposed an Internal Purchase Scheme
by which all surplus paddy was collected by the Government in order to

---

[1] Press supplement to commemorate the first anniversary of the Paddy
Lands Act - Ceylon Daily News, 2nd March 1959.

assure a minimum supply of rice to consumers. After the war the policy
of supporting domestic agriculture was continued with a view to achieving
a high level of food production domestically. Thus, in 1948, the Internal
Purchase Scheme was replaced by a guaranteed price scheme.

The guaranteed price scheme assures the farmers   a "fair price" by
the government irrespective of open market prices prevailing in the
country or even in the world market. It operates on a voluntary basis
and the producer is free to decide whether or not to surrender his
produce to the government at the fixed price or to sell it to any other
buyer.[1] Under the scheme therefore the producer will have a buyer of last
resort whenever the open market price drops below the price fixed under
the scheme.

The guaranteed price scheme as it has operated in Sri Lanka seeks:

(a) to stimulate production of paddy, and thereby replace imports
by local production, with self-sufficiency as the ultimate goal;

(b) to increase the incomes and welfare of the rural population by
ensuring the producers a fair price and a ready market; and

(c) to ensure an equitable distribution of rice on ration among
the consumers in the country.

Policy makers have thus assumed that the price guaranteed under the
scheme will act as an incentive to increased production. It thus constitutes one of the major components in the "package deal" offered to farmers
which includes improved seed and technology, extension, credit and low
priced agricultural inputs.

The second objective aims at improving farm incomes. Given the
importance of paddy cultivation in rural areas (paddy occupies the largest
acreage of any single crop, its cultivation is still the central activity
in most villages and provides perhaps the largest amount of employment
in the agricultural sector) a guaranteed price can directly help to
improve farm incomes. The third objective we have discussed elsewhere in

----

[1] However, in 1973, the Paddy Marketing Board was given monopoly
powers to buy all the marketable surpluses of paddy from the farmers in
order to assure consumers their weekly ration. However, this attempt
proved unsuccessful and the restrictions on paddy/rice trade were
removed in 1975.

the context of the net food subsidy. At present the Paddy Marketing Board (PMB) purchases paddy under the GPS largely through village co-operatives and to some extent through authorised purchasers. The paddy is issued to private and co-operative mills by the PMB and the rice is delivered to the Food Commissioner's Department which then distributes this rice through co-operatives to the consumers.

The scheme has come to be used principally to supply rice for the ration. The Draft Agricultural Development Plan (1971-1977) states, "Since the Guaranteed Price Scheme is now a means for feeding the rationing scheme, the most important intention is that it should be capable of buying a higher and higher percentage of the local production to eliminate imports. This is the central problem of the Guaranteed Price Scheme for paddy in coming years." This has been reflected in several changes made to the scheme so far. Quality specifications were lowered in the late 1960s to allow paddy with refraction rates of up to 12 per cent and moisture content as high as 17 per cent to be accepted. Another change was the suspension of crop lists on which paddy was purchased under the GPS. According to the earlier system only genuine farmers could sell their produce under the scheme. However, after suspending the crop lists any person, whether he be a paddy producer or not, was able to sell paddy to the Government at the GPS price.

Despite an increasing guaranteed price the amount of paddy purchased by the government has progressively declined over the last few years which suggests some inefficiency in procurement. Among possible major factors are a number of shortcomings at the co-operatives, the village agents of the PMB, such as insufficient liquid cash to pay producers, delays and the congestion caused by lack of storage space, staff, and transport facilities and delays caused by the new methods of testing and grading paddy.

Farmers have also been reluctant to sell their paddy to co-operatives for fear that their unpaid loans will be deducted from the proceeds. Producers may thus accept even a slightly lower price from private traders. Possibly the loss from the difference between the two is more than offset by the convenience of dealing with private traders, who are concerned less with quality specifications and above all buy at the farm gate paying spot cash. This means that the price advantage of the scheme does not accrue to the producer since the middleman may finally sell his paddy under the GPS.

In reviewing the operation of the scheme a number of points must be remembered. One is that producers have also been eligible for rationed rice.

Normally, therefore, when rationed rice was cheap, and the quantity issued per person substantial, farmers would sell more paddy. In this event the GPS price would be higher than the open market price. Then it follows logically that government would get more paddy, if the production had not declined due to adverse weather conditions. The upward trend in GPS purchases during the 1954-66 period was mainly due to this. Similarly, when the price of rationed rice is increased we could expect the reverse situation. The available evidence suggests that this happened in 1953. In that year the Government increased the price of rationed rice from Rs. 0.25 cts. to Rs. 0.70 cts. a measure. The volume of paddy purchased declined from 1.3 to 0.3 million bushels.[1]

In addition the price and availability of wheat flour can be decisive. In 1973, when the Government restricted wheat flour imports, despite all monopoly powers given to PMB the open market price for paddy went up to unprecedented levels. In January 1973, the open market price for a bushel of paddy ranged from Rs. 50-60 even in Polonnaruwa, one of the major surplus producing areas. The GPS price at that time was only Rs. 33. The open market price again declined when the Government allowed imports of flour into the country in 1976.

Our general impression nevertheless is that the GPS has generally been higher than the cost of production in most areas and that during most years it has been higher than the open market price. Hence the impact of the GPS on the adoption of better management practices cannot be ruled out though the degree of its impact may certainly be questioned. Above all during the period of 1964-1970 the rate of increase of rice yields was very high, 4.8 per cent annually.

Assuming that the GPS has had an impact on promoting technological progress in paddy cultivation, a more pertinent question to be asked would be "Who has responded to the price incentive?".

Firstly, the following table indicates the adoption of some important farm practices.

---

[1] A similar tendency was experienced in 1967 when the Government reduced the ration by 50 per cent (to 2 lbs of rice). Purchases through the guaranteed price scheme dropped from 28.0 million bushels in 1966 to 13.4 million bushels in 1967.

Table 4: Adoption of some important farm practices

	Polonnaruwa	Kegalle Kandy	Colombo
Farmers who used certified seed (per cent)	40	10	7
Area transplanted (per cent)	88	93	16
Farmers who applied agro-chemicals (per cent)	79	67	63
Farmers who applied some kind of fertilizer (per cent)	95	93	62
Amount of nitrogen applied (lbs/ac)	107	63	36
Average yield (bu/ac)	76	48	32

Source: A.S. Ranatunga and W.A.T. Abeysekera, "Profitability and Resource Characteristics in Paddy Farming", ARTI, Colombo, 1977.

It is clear that the package of new technology has been adopted on a large scale mainly in the areas favoured with better water supply conditions and favourable tenurial arrangements. Polonnaruwa, which is favoured in both aspects has a higher rate of adoption than Kandy-Kegalle (Mid-Country Wet Zone) which is less favoured in terms of tenurial conditions (tenancy, micro-holdings). The majority of the farmers in the Low-Country Wet Zone and the Dry Zone rainfed or minor tankfed areas are unable to take up the new technology and therefore to benefit from the GPS. The difference between Polonnaruwa and Colombo is obvious.

It is also clear that the marketable surplus of paddy available with a producer determines the use he can make of the GPS. This depends to some extent on the quantity of rationed rice issued, as well as on the level of production. In any event the majority of holdings are very small. In 1962 about 43 per cent of total paddy holdings were a part of total holdings themselves less than two-and-a-half acres in extent with the paddy area under one acre. Only some 40 bushels of paddy can be expected per annum from holdings of around one acre. It is highly unlikely that this group would have any genuine excess paddy to sell, implying limited gains from a guaranteed price scheme.

This position becomes clearer when we consider the disproportionate collections under the GPS from different districts. Polonnaruwa, Hambantota Amparai, Trincomalee and Balticaloa, where most of the paddy holdings are over two acres in extent and are served by major irrigation schemes contribute up to 75 per cent of GPS collections, whereas nine of the Wet Zone districts plus Jaffna contribute only 15-20 per cent of GPS collections.

A recent study by the Agrarian Research and Training Institute[1] showed that in two surplus paddy producing districts, Polonnaruwa and Hambantota, farmers sold 70 per cent and 55 per cent of their production respectively during the study period (Maha 1976/77). In absolute terms these sales amounted to 191 and 109 bushels respectively. But in contrast, in the Wet Zone areas, Colombo and Kandy-Kegalle, the amount sold per farm averaged only 3-8 bushels per farm (Table 5).

The authors concluded that "small quantities of paddy offered for sale per farm ... does not constitute a real surplus production but merely a case of 'hunger sales' ... it follows that the average producers of this area would reap only marginal benefits from the existing price support programmes ... In this context ... any given increase in the Guaranteed Price Scheme would result in a differential impact on cash incomes of the producers in surplus and deficit areas."[2]

Table 5: Quantity disposed as a percentage of total output (per cent)

Mode of disposal	Polonnaruwa	Hambantota	Kegalle-Kandy	Colombo
a. Sales	70	55	22	13
b. Payments in kind (land rent, loan repayments, hired labour and draught power)	3	21	15	9
c. Home retention	27	24	63	78
Total output per farm				
Percentage	100	100	100	100
Bushels	273	197	36	23

Source: A.S. Ranatunga and W.A.T. Abeysekera, op. cit.

Table 5 also shows the importance of payments in kind to land owners, draught power owners and hired labour, in determining the marketable surplus in various districts.

----

[1] A.S. Ranatunga and W.A.T. Abeysekera, op. cit.

[2] Ibid.

Input programmes

Successive governments have adopted a number of incentive schemes to encourage paddy production. They include such inter-connected measures as:

(i) Supply of credit at subsidised interest rates;

(ii) Supply of fertilizer at a subsidised price and

(iii) Supply of seed paddy and agro-chemicals.

These input supply programmes had the dual objective of inducing farmers to adopt a package of improved practices and improving and stabilising their incomes particularly by relieving them of their indebtedness to money-lenders.[1]

Government intervention in the supply of essential inputs to the paddy sector dates back to the early 1950s at least. No doubt these programmes have contributed to increased output. However, doubts have been expressed as to whether such programmes have in fact benefitted the large majority of farmers, especially small-holders and tenants.

The first government agricultural credit scheme began in 1947. The Department of Agrarian Services took over this scheme in 1957 and wrote off all overdue loans taken before 1958. The volume of credit granted was also increased from Rs. 75/- to Rs. 250 per acre. In 1967 a New Agricultural Credit Scheme to be administered by the People's Bank was introduced, once again waiving all defaults (one-third of all loans taken were in default and one-third of co-operatives had defaulted). By 1972 both utilisation and repayment had declined and once again in 1973 a new scheme, the Comprehensive Rural Credit Scheme, was launched, this time too bringing defaulters back into the scheme. In 1977, by which time defaults had increased, agricultural credit was given to all farmers irrespective of whether or not they had defaulted. The current agricultural credit scheme is operated mainly through the network of village co-operatives and to some extent through co-operative rural banks and the Bank of Ceylon[2] branches in

---

[1] Crop insurance is another programme which has been introduced.

[2] With the establishment in 1973 of Agricultural Productivity Committees, one per each Village Council area, a branch of the Bank of Ceylon was also established in each Productivity Centre.

rural areas. The Central Bank provides a refinancing facility of 75 per cent of the unrecovered credit. Agricultural credit is granted without any form of security. Before granting a fresh loan only the past repayment record of a farmer is considered.

Table 6 gives the national picture on the provision of agricultural credit and amounts repaid. Despite a disappointing record of repayment successive governments have extended the credit programme. Unpaid loans have been written off whenever credit utilisation decreased. However, like the rice ration, credit has now become virtually a political issue, its withdrawal likely to seriously affect the vote. This credit policy has often been criticised for liberalising credit without adequate follow-up of recoveries, lack of supervision and granting of credit with no relation to specific production programmes.[1] Nevertheless, the role of credit in improving the production and income levels of the small farmer and particularly protecting him from the money lender is important. But has the credit programme achieved these objectives?

Even after 30 years of credit schemes the majority of farmers continue to depend on non-institutional sources of lending, although credit is granted without any form of security and at a low rate of interest. One

Table 6: Position of loans granted as at 31.12.77 (in millions of rupees)

Year	Amount granted	Total repayments	Amounts due	Amounts not paid	Percentage repayments
67/68	72,712	62,633	10,026	10,026	86.0
68/69	55,669	36,598	18,707	19,071	65.7
69/70	51,705	29,222	22,393	33,483	56.5
70/71	29,273	18,014	11,259	11,259	61.8
71/72	30,623	20,585	10,017	10,038	67.2
72/73	28,445	18,563	9,702	9,702	65.3
73/74	109,049	57,570	51,479	51,479	52.8
74/75	77,063	35,208	41,857	41,855	45.7
75/76	56,367	28,802	27,529	27,565	51.1
76/77	73,151	20,928	46,461	52,223	28.6
77/78 Maha only	221,586	31	-	221,555	-
Total	805,463	328,154	249,425	477,309	40.7

Source: Economic Review, Colombo, January 1978.

[1] J.M. Gunadasa, "A Review of Planning for Paddy Production", Modern Ceylon Studies, Vol. 3, (2), 1972.

study has recently shown that "of the 5 areas studied institutional credit channelled through co-operatives is important only in Polonnaruwa and Hambantota ... . In comparison to institutional sources, private lenders play an equal or perhaps a more dominant role as creditors to paddy farmers in both these districts."[1] Both these districts are also surplus paddy producing areas. However, in deficit areas like Colombo, Kandy and Kegalle, the same study found that less than one per cent of farmers in the sample had used production credit. In other districts private sources of lending play the predominant role as suppliers of credit.[2]

A review of the institutional credit scheme shows that it is the larger farmers who make greatest use of it. Information available for two districts shows this tendency clearly in both a surplus and a deficit area.

Table 7: Institutional borrowing by size of operational holding

| Size of holding (acres) | Per cent of borrowers in each size class | |
	Kandy	Polonnaruwa
Up to 0.50	-	
0.50 - 1.00	15	40
1.00 - 2.00	54	
2.00 - 4.00	62	54
4.00 - 6.00	67	56
6.00 - 8.00		64
8.00 - 10.00	89	66
Over 10.00		75

Source: ARTI, The Agrarian Situation ..., op. cit.

Similarly, Table 8 shows that borrowings from institutional sources by tenants are also generally low compared to other tenurial categories.

The Kandy report of the Agrarian Situation summarised this position as follows: "... the average amount of loan from all sources per borrower for the owner group is high compared to all other tenurial categories ... borrowers among owners meet a greater proportion of their credit requirements from co-operatives ... the average amount of loan per

---

[1] A.S. Ranatunga and W.A.T. Abeysekera, op. cit.

[2] See for example ARTI, The Agrarian Situation ..., op. cit., where it states that in Anuradhapura, "There is a heavy dependence on private sources of credit. The largest proportion of borrowers (58 per cent) relied on such sources for their loan."

Table 8: Institutional borrowings according to tenurial status

Tenurial category	Per cent of borrowers in each status group		
	Kandy	Polonnaruwa	Anuradhapura
Owners	64	68	31
Owner-tenants	83	46	25
Tenant-owners	60	50	-
Tenants	50	-	-
Others	-	31	18

Source: ARTI, The Agrarian Situation ..., op. cit.

tenant is very small and the tenant group utilises private sources more than the co-operatives."[1] This unequal access to credit stems from the power of the relatively large farmers in economic, social and political fields in their communities. In addition larger farmers, through their superior risk bearing ability, are less hesitant to adopt new management practices. They have greater access to other inputs and technical advice and are able to invest in agriculture all the credit they obtain. Similarly they hold or have greater access to important positions in such village institutions as co-operatives which are responsible for disbursing institutional credit.

However, all the three study locations showed that in the 1971/72 Maha season a larger proportion of owners than of tenants repaid their co-operative and bank loans. In Anuradhapura the repayment rate for owners was 62 per cent, in Polonnaruwa 76 per cent and Kandy 86 per cent. For tenants however, repayments in Anuradhapura amounted to 50 per cent, in Kandy 67 per cent and in Polonnaruwa 33 per cent. Not only is the tenants' capacity to repay reduced by their paying a large part of their yield as rent, but they are also more dependent on non-institutional sources of borrowing and are compelled to repay these loans earlier. In all the above study locations private sources of credit had a greater recovery rate, partly because the high interest rates charged by some non-institutional lenders also compel the borrowers to repay early.

Similar information is not available by size of holdings. A Central Bank study noted that repayments have not followed a uniform pattern ... according to size of area cultivated.[2] However, ARTI studies have shown

[1] ARTI, The Agrarian Situation ... op. cit.

[2] Central Bank of Ceylon, "Survey of Defaulters in the Repayment of New Agricultural Loans", Colombo, 1972.

that in Kandy and Anuradhapura a sizeable proportion of farmers with
comparatively large holdings have outstanding co-operative loans.
Whether these farmers, who normally should have a higher repayment capacity, avoided repayment intentionally is unknown. However, similar instances reported elsewhere suggest this. Khan and Gunadasa[1] found that
in the Beminiwatta area of Kegalle District many larger farmers avoided
repayment of institutional loans.

But the medium-term agricultural credit from banks may have contributed more to widening income disparities between large and small
farmers. Credit given for the purchase of tractors, water pumps, and
sprayers, would go into the hands of larger farmers. Such credit is given
on concessionary rates but the banks require a guarantee of a high asset
value as security, and then lend 75 per cent of the cost of the article.
For example, the retail price of a four-wheel tractor was Rs. 15,600 in
early 1968. This increased to Rs. 21,000 in May 1968 and in 1978 to
around Rs. 110,000. Very few small farmers could afford around Rs. 30,000
of their own cash as a deposit to purchase a four-wheel tractor.

Clearly the larger and more affluent farmers benefit most from
the subsidised credit programme. They can invest all the credit they
obtain to improve production and also benefit indirectly by relending
(either in cash or in kind, such as fertilizer to tenants) institutional
credit to poorer farmers or by avoiding repayment. The small operators
and tenants generally borrow less since their risk bearing ability and the
capacity to repay are both weak. Even if they borrow many of them are
compelled to use a part of the credit for consumption. The productive
investment of what remains is hampered by the lack of technical advice
and access to other inputs.[2]

A further support programme is the fertilizer subsidy scheme introduced in 1950-51. In 1962-63 the scheme was revised to give a 50 per cent

_____

[1] A.A. Khan and J.M. Gunadasa, Small Farmer Credit, ARTI, Colombo, 1973.

[2] Narayanasamy et al., Role of Rural Organizations in Rural Development
in Sri Lanka, ARTI, Colombo, 1977.

subsidy to all paddy cultivators buying fertilizer for cash. Credit sales had a one-third subsidy. This system continued until 1974, when the subsidy on fertilizer was removed altogether. It was re-introduced in 1975; in November 1977 it was increased to 75 per cent for cash, but it was brought down to 50 per cent in the middle of 1978.

Paddy cultivators as a whole reacted quickly to these changes with increasing use of fertilizers in 1964 and declining levels recorded in 1975. But the discriminatory subsidy policy followed over the years raises serious implications for the welfare aspects of the subsidy scheme because a higher rate of subsidy was allowed for more affluent farmers paying cash for their fertilizers.

Regional differences in fertilizer use are relevant here. Ranatunga and Abeysekera have found that except in Colombo, where part-time farming is predominant, in all other locations (i.e. Polonnaruwa, Hambantota and Kegalle-Kandy) about 95 per cent of the farmers used some kind of fertilizer for paddy, although there were significant differences in amounts of nitrogen applied. In Polonnaruwa the per acre application of nitrogen was 107 lbs. It was 66, 63 and 36 lbs per acre respectively in Hambantota, Kegalle-Kandy and Colombo. This picture is adequately representative of the national situation. From the fertilizer scheme also, the farmers of the surplus producing areas are likely to benefit more than their counterparts in other areas.

Ranatunga and Abeysekera concluded that in Polonnaruwa the level of fertilizer applied approximated to the dosage recommended by the Department of Agriculture. However, this average for the entire district conceals the variations within the district, and more particularly among farmers with different sizesof operational holdings. Table 9 gives a clear indication how farmers operating holdings of different sizes benefit from the subsidy scheme. The table shows a high proportion of operators in the 10 acres plus group, as well as those in the 4-6 acres group, made 3 applications of fertilizer. Fewer farmers in the smaller size classes in fact make full use of the subsidy.

Moreover, the same study shows that within Polonnaruwa, while 76 per cent of the farmers in major irrigation schemes applied fertilizer only 38 per cent of farmers in the minor irrigation schemes did so. Hence, even within the Dry Zone the benefits of the fertilizer subsidy scheme mostly help:

(i) the operators of larger holdings and;

(ii) farmers in the major irrigation schemes whose holdings are not only larger but who have reliable irrigation allowing double cropping and an assured yield.

Table 9: Application of fertilizer according to size of holding - Polonnaruwa District

Size of holding (acres)	Number of applications - per cent in size group		
	At least once		Three times
	Farmers	Extent (acres)	Farmers
Up to 2.00	42	32	8
2.00 - 4.00	74	78	46
4.00 - 6.00	86	83	62
6.00 - 8.00	78	78	50
8.00 - 10.00	85	80	54
Over 10.00	86	91	71
TOTAL	78	80	51

Source: ARTI, The Agrarian Situation ..., op.cit.

Generally the maximum potential benefits of fertilizer application are rarely obtained by the small farmer since he lacks adequate technical advice and is often unable to get his limited quantity of fertilizer in time.

Tenancy would not appear to discourage the use of fertilizer. In Kandy[1] and Kegalle,[2] both with a high incidence of tenancy, data indicate no marked difference between owner and tenant operators in fertilizer application. But in most Wet Zone areas tenants still continue to pay 50 per cent of the crop to the landlord. This latter provides fertilizer and recovers the cost with interest at harvest. Hence most tenants apply fertilizer provided by the landlord and most landlords provide it because they will also finally benefit.

---

[1] ARTI, The Agrarian Situation ..., op. cit.

[2] Ibid.

A further programme concerns the distribution of paddy seed. The Department of Agriculture does not undertake to supply all the seed paddy required by farmers, but offers to replace it once in 3 or 4 years. Therefore, from the farmers' point of view, the supply of certified seed paddy is always below demand. This often implies injustice to small farmers since more influential and larger farmers are likely to obtain the better seeds from the extension workers.

The use of agro-chemicals in plant protection has not been officially encouraged in Sri Lanka. The import and distribution of chemicals is unsubsidised and has remained largely in the hands of private dealers although some co-operatives also distribute them. However, with the spread of NHYVS their use has increased quickly.

Unlike fertilizers, the application of agro-chemicals requires spraying equipment generally owned by private traders and larger farmers. The number of sprayers owned by the village cultivation committees is limited and their use monopolised by the larger farmers. Most small farmers have therefore to depend on private owners who are very often also the agro-chemical dealers themselves. Small farmers' dependence on these sources has the following consequences:

(i) The dealer generally sells what is available with him and perhaps not the right kind of chemical.

(ii) The dealer provides the sprayers only if the chemicals are bought from him and of course at a higher price.[1]

(iii) The sprayer owners are generally not willing to go to small individual plots.

A further difficulty faced by small farmers is that the chemicals are generally available only in larger bottles. Most small farmers need only small quantities and few can afford to invest in a large bottle. Thus he overcomes this difficulty by depending on the private dealer for both the equipment and the chemicals which often results in a higher unit price.

To summarise this section it seems generally clear that while most input supply programmes have helped to increase paddy production at the national level, at the regional and farm level a greater share of the benefits are being absorbed by larger farmers and to some extent by input suppliers.

---

[1] Hameed, et al., op. cit.

While there are physical, agronomic, economic and socio-institutional
constraints to an equal distribution of the benefits from these programmes,
any improvement in this situation requires improving the "delivery mechan-
isms" of such inputs through institutional arrangements more representative
of and sympathetic towards the weaker sections of the farming community.

Irrigation and resettlement programmes

Successive governments have followed a policy of irrigation development
and resettlement. These programmes aimed at increasing food production and
had the strong social objective of relieving landlessness in the overcrowded Wet Zone.[1] These programmes were a major field of investment and
occupied a primary place in development programmes.

Resettlement projects in the Dry Zone, usually referred to as colonisation schemes, are essentially based on the provision of irrigation
facilities for paddy cultivation.[2] Most of these schemes consist largely
of the renovated irrigation works or ancient irrigation schemes integrated
with modern works as the Mahaweli project.[3]

Most allottees were selected from among the landless persons with
larger families from the Wet Zone areas. However, landless families
from the neighbouring Dry Zone villages were also absorbed into the
schemes. Between 1935 and 1948 around 1,470 allottees were settled on
some 12,600 acres of land. However, after Independence colonisation progressed
at a faster rate. Between 1948 and 1968 some 81,730 allottees on 587,000
acres were settled in various parts of the Dry Zone.

In order to accommodate a greater number of settlers in the schemes,
the allotment size had also been progressively reduced from 8 acres
(5 irrigated and 3 highland) to 3 acres (2 acres irrigated and 1 acre
highland). The present allocation in the Mahaweli project is 2.75 acres
(2.5 acres irrigated and 0.25 acre homestead). As another measure of cost
reduction, the free house earlier provided to the colonist was withdrawn
in the late 1960s and instead a nominal payment is made to assist him to
build his own house.

---

[1] Other objectives included the creation of a class of landowning independent peasants and the recreation of the past glories of the Rajarata,
then known as the granary of the East.

[2] There are 3 main types of scheme: multi-purpose (including power
generation), major irrigation and minor irrigation projects.

[3] Some schemes such as Gal Oya, Udawalawe and Rajangana are entirely
new in conception and execution.

Doubts have often been expressed on the contribution of resettlement programmes particularly because the direct impact of colonisation in solving the food and employment problems had been far less than anticipated and proportionately still less than the investment made on them. Resettlement programmes have opened around 700,000 acres of jungle land for agricultural production and human settlement and have directly benefitted over 80,000 landless families. This would have meant that around 160,000 people have been provided with primary employment in agriculture. Most of these people were the landless in the overcrowded areas of the Wet Zone. Today, thanks to resettlement, they obtain significantly higher incomes than the families in their original villages. But the annual rate of settlement has not been high.

The greatest contribution of resettlement programmes has been to increase rice production. This rose from some 30 million bushels in 1952 to 80 million bushels in 1977 and there is no doubt that because of resettlement the Dry Zone has been converted into a rice surplus area.

But these benefits have been realised at a very high cost. The irrigation and resettlement programmes have been highly capital-intensive. The cost of settling one family was as high as Rs. 21,000 in Gal Oya (1965) and remained around Rs. 16,000 for other major schemes. The foreign exchange share of major schemes has been close to 55 per cent and for colonisation 75 per cent. Most schemes had a long gestation period ranging from 10 to 18 years. The majority of these schemes have been low yielding, often not paying back their full cost even after 50 years. With the project costs amortised over 50 years the benefit cost ratio worked out to only 0.56 for Mahakanadarawa and 0.67 for Rajangana.[1] For Gal Oya, one of the oldest and largest, it was only 0.5.[2] Highland plots have generally remained underutilised or even neglected. Irrigated land has been exclusively utilised for paddy cultivation. Inefficient land and water use has been a major cause of their failure to further improve food production in the country. Similarly the employment created is only some 6 to 7 per cent of the average annual increase in the workforce.

The high cost of the schemes was partly due to poor planning and phasing of construction. Many schemes dragged on over long periods leading to high

---

[1] Department of National Planning, "The Short Term Implementation Programme", Colombo, 1962.

[2] "Report of the Gal Oya Project Evaluation Committee", Colombo, 1970.

construction costs, interest payable on capital and the denial of benefits from the schemes had they been completed earlier. Rajangana scheme
took 18 years for completion. If it had been completed in 8 years, the
loss due to delay would have been equal to the full cost of the work.[1]

The colony land use system itself was neither based on sound agricultural principles nor on economic principles of putting both land and
water to maximum use. The scope for raising production and incomes
through agricultural intensification and diversification has never been
fully realised. The extension services were woefully inadequate to realise
these aims (most colonists simply transferred the agricultural practices
they were used to in their own villages) and the supporting services for
input deliveries and effective farmer organisation for promoting agricultural development were weak or lacking. The colony layout itself
(ribbon type settlements) precluded the development of effective farmer
co-operation. Constrained by such deficiencies, most colonies had to operate
at a low level of efficiency.

However, the indirect benefits of the resettlement programmes are certainly significant. The programmes have brought about a considerable
shift in the country's population. In the North Central Province and
Eastern Province where colonisation has been heaviest, population grew threefold from 1946 to 1976 compared to its doubling in the country as a whole.

Apart from official settlers the Dry Zone has also attracted both
considerable numbers of encroachers and migrant labour. The encroachers
as a group, engaged mainly in highland crop production, make a substantial
contribution to the production of many subsidiary food crops particularly
pulses, dry grains and chillies. They have, over the years, evolved
the required skills to make highland cultivation under rainfed conditions
(an alternative development for larger areas of the Dry Zone which cannot
be irrigated) a more profitable venture.

Resettlement programmes have also helped to reduce, even in a
limited way, the development of a very serious agrarian situation in certain
parts of the Wet Zone and helped to arrest the increase in slum development
in Wet Zone cities. Colonisation has always been a politically more neutral

---

[1] Department of National Planning, op. cit.

solution to the problems of landlessness in the Wet Zone than, for example, land reform, which would have been less costly but more sensitive. It was also attractive because the impact of settlement programmes was widespread as colonists could be drawn from different parts of the country and also resettled in different areas. The creation of a class of independent land-owning peasants was also particularly attractive to most governments as it helped to create a solid conservative rural base. However, this political attraction of the resettlement programmes gave them a strong social welfare bias and a complete lack of cost consciousness.

Resettlement programmes have created imbalances both at an inter-regional level and within the Dry Zone. These schemes have created a class of well-to-do farmers who have not only received a fully developed holding and other amenities at no cost[1] but also continue to absorb a high proportion of benefits - from most of the incentive prices and subsidies - offered by the State to the peasant sector. As noted earlier the colonists with larger holdings (with assured irrigation supplies) are in a better position to make use of credit, of subsidised inputs and are also able to benefit more from the incentive paddy price. Thus the colonists are among the highest income earners in the rural sector and absorb a large slice of government subsidy programmes.[2] As a result income disparities have increased between colonists on the one hand and the peasants in their original villages of the Wet Zone and adjacent small tank-based settlements in the Dry Zone on the other, and between colonists and encroachers. The latter cannot bene-fit from such government programmes as credit, because they are not regis-tered cultivators, and from the subsidies and incentive prices which are offered mainly to paddy which they do not cultivate.

Nor has the objective of creating a single class of independent peasant proprietors in the Dry Zone colonies been achieved. Evidence sug-gests that increasing number of colonists are either losing their lands or leasing/mortgaging them to richer farmers or trader/money-lenders. Hidden

---

[1] The irrigation rate charged in major schemes is only Rs. 5 per acre. This represents less than one-third of the actual cost of maintenance of these schemes. Even this is usually not paid.

[2] Until mid-1977, when the rice ration was withdrawn from those families earning a monthly income of Rs. 300, colonists benefitted from all the food subsidies as well.

fragmentation and tenancy are becoming a reality in most colonisation schemes.[1] Many of the landless who received allotments in the colonies lacked managerial skill and in some cases even agricultural know-how. Without proper training and extension many of them were unable to emerge from the poverty trap. Further, the usual feature of indebtedness to private sources still continues. Even in the more prosperous colonisation schemes of Polonnaruwa 30 per cent of the farmers borrowed from private sources in 1976-77.[2] Thus many colonists still depend on private creditors, tractor-owners and input suppliers for their farming needs. These people are likely to absorb a good portion of the benefits from incentive prices and subsidy schemes. They are also gradually buying up colony lands or obtaining them on lease or mortgage, the owners being thus converted into tenants and labourers.

The second and third generations of the original settlers are now often faced with problems of landlessness and unemployment. Some of them receive lands in new colonies but others become encroachers or labourers. The long-term needs of a growing population in the colonies had little place in the original planning. Thus, the expensive resettlement programme was clearly considered more as a social welfare exercise with a high degree of immediate political gains built in. The negative developments noted are the inevitable consequences of an approach which failed to combine welfare with growth.

---

[1] ARTI, The Agrarian Situation ..., op. cit., Hameed et al., op. cit. and A.O. Ellman, et al., "Land Settlement in Sri Lanka, A Review of Major Writings", ARTI, Colombo, 1976.

[2] A.S. Ranatunga and W.A.T. Abeysekera, op. cit.

CHAPTER 7
Participation, Administration and Representation[1]

Introduction

    This introductory section aims to provide a framework which
will help in appreciating the role and relevance of other phenomena.
It deals with three sets of relationships; control within the
community (usually the legitimising of property or employment relationships and the provision of a framework to permit gradual change)
relations of community members (villagers) to the central government
(representation) and relations of villagers to central government officials
(administration). For a study of basic needs the importance of the
relationships is the following: they affect the speed at which any community
is joined to any given network supplying basic needs services, they determine the efficiency with which outside resources are brought to the
village and used within the village and they determine the distribution
of the benefits created by the intrusion of those resources.

    The three relationships are very closely interlinked. Control
within the village determines the means of access to central government
officials and easy access in turn gives influence within the village.
Correspondingly, the central government administration can legitimise
and delegitimise control within the village. The administration and the
representatives (i.e. members of the central legislature) can determine
the distribution of basic needs services (and many other inputs) throughout
the country.[2] Political representatives have, of course, in recent years
been able to do much more, i.e. to promote the fortune of one group of
households against that of another. It is interesting here to note
that this activity on the part of representatives has often been
compatible with the continuation of methods of control and of traditional
property and employment relationships within the village. This we noted

---

[1] This chapter draws partly on the ILO-SIDA report, "District level
planning in Sri Lanka", written by G. Edgren, P. Richards and J. Majeres.

[2] Note that before representatives became powerful the estates had
power of this kind.

in discussing the regulation of tenancy in the previous chapter. As a
result the role of representatives is therefore more likely to lead to
"factionalism" than radical change. Factionalism, and regular shifts in
the party in power in Colombo, however, is not compatible with the
continuing and uninterrupted influence usually of one individual or
family. However, factionalism requires the existence of well-balanced
interest groups in order to arise in the first place. It might therefore
be claimed that party politics in Sri Lanka have been incompatible with the
old Village Headman system and conversely that party politics ensure that
the Grama Sevaka[1] often remains uninfluential.

The basic needs networks referred to are of two kinds. One is
fairly insensitive to power relationships within the village and the other
not. The first includes such matters as road linkages, schools, post-
offices and hospitals. The way these are sited can, of course, favour powerful over weak groups causing greater or less inconvenience, waste of time
in travelling, expense, etc. However, it seems fair to state that these
are community services and disputes about their location take place between
and not within geographically limited community groups. Furthermore these
are all services with high running costs and are therefore beyond the
capacity of the community to maintain, even if the community could assist
in the original construction. Therefore, in order to have such facilities
influence is needed with central government departments and public
corporations. And, it might be added, whatever the influence given to
local bodies by decentralised budgeting procedures the need for this
linkage between villagers and the central government will remain. Scarce
resources need rationing and rationing requires priorities.

The other kind of basic needs network is different. This kind
brings fertilizers and seeds to the farm gate and provides or
assists with irrigation facilities. Here the representative can only
play a determining role through some intermediary and, of course, in
recent years that intermediary was created by allowing MPs the right
to nominate members of the old Agricultural Productivity Committees
and Janatha Committees. In other situations the main determining

---

[1] Village Headman.

relationship was between the government administration and such village bodies as the Co-operative or even the Rural Development Society. But the leadership of these organisations was, and is, often seen as a stepping stone to party-political office and as one of the power bases which a representative needs to secure. As a general rule the result would be that the new resources created or brought into the village would be subject to the same intra-village control as those that already existed.[1] In these matters, therefore, the administration would relate to various formal and informal village leaders, who are most likely to be business men or successful owner-cultivators. However, it is important to note that such bodies as Co-operative Societies and Rural Development Societies have often led a rather shadowy existence, becoming inoperative and re-appearing a few years later. This has presumably allowed them to avoid some of the problems of factionalism but it has also considerably reduced their influence. Given that Rural Development Societies are the nearest thing to a democratically elected single village level body (which Village Committees are not, and co-operative membership requires a fee) this may have been a great loss. In principle, as we saw in the previous chapter, the distribution of portable inputs into agriculture was influenced through the Co-operative Society and that of infrastructural inputs could have been, but rarely was, influenced by the Rural Development Society.

In many ways it is fair to assume that the central government working through its administration has supported the status quo so far as control procedures within the village are concerned. The Kandyan Peasantry Commission[2] stressed how the administration was far more successful in protecting the forests against encroachment and felling than Ande cultivators or Nindagam tenants against high rent shares. And, of course, the land reform laws generally left untouched village land ownership. But, firstly, the government did replace Village Headmen, and Vel Vidanes (irrigation headmen), and therefore did remove some sources of village

---

[1] Village level complaints apparently abound of Rural Development Society officers having roads constructed to their private houses and of voluntary labour schemes only benefiting larger farmers, see ARTI, The role of rural organisations in rural development in Sri Lanka, Colombo, 1977.

[2] Sessional Paper no. XVIII of 1951, Report of the Kandyan Peasantry Commission.

power. Secondly, government "interference" has ranged from the very
extreme, i.e. intensive area development projects on colonisation schemes
to the very limited, i.e. in many "squatting" communities. An interesting
example of very far-reaching government intervention is given by Amarasiri
de Silva[1] describing the supply of motorised fishing boats to a coastal
community. These were passed over, on very favourable terms, to deep-sea
fishermen, hitherto one of the poorest groups (fishing inshore was far
more profitable). A totally new set of people came to prominence but
many, in turn, lost out to money lenders and others with the ready money to
purchase complementary inputs not supplied by government. In this case
the social structure changed less, finally, than the government had intended but the government had channelled in a very considerable amount of
resources to the community, specifically to a less prosperous group.
But sea is not land.

However, while intra-village relations may have remained fairly
stable in recent years the nexus of "village-representative-administration"
has not. A number of innovations have been tried out with the intention
of bringing the government officialdom closer to the local community with
the representative as intermediary. These have occurred in the context of
the Divisional Development Council programme (with some very close echoes in
the administration of certain lands taken over in the 1972 Land Reform),
in the Decentralised Budget and in other attempts at District and Village-
level planning. Before discussing these innovations a few basic statistics
on administrative and local government areas are required.

With a population of 12.7 mln. in 1971, Sri Lanka has 22 districts,
168 electorates, 242 AGA[2] divisions, 549 Village Committees, and perhaps
22,000 villages, with also 83 town councils, 38 urban and 12 municipal
councils. Only the last of these are outside the Kachcheri[3] system of
administration although it would seem eminently sensible to integrate

---

[1] M.W. Amarasiri de Silva, "Structural change in a coastal fishing
community in Southern Sri Lanka", Marga, Vol. 4, No. 2, 1977.

[2] Assistant Government Agent. The AGA division is the smallest unit
with an administrative service officer at its head.

[3] The district administrative headquarters.

urban councils (many of which are larger than some municipal councils)
into the municipal council system. In 1971 municipal councils accounted
for some 10 per cent of the total population and urban councils a further
6 per cent. Town councils had some 7 per cent. A Village Committee area
thus averaged around 18,000 persons in 1971 and a village averaged some
450 persons. In 1977 some 3,200 village level Rural Development Societies
were registered, at least one half of which had existed for more than 20
years and 80 per cent for more than 10 years, according to a survey by
the Rural Development Department. The present Government's intention is
to raise the number of RDSs to some 20,000 or, within reason, one for
every major village. There would then be 36 RDSs per Village Committee
area (not that any legal or organic relation exists between RDSs and
Village Committees) and over 90 per AGA's division. There would be
some 150 RDSs per electorate.

Divisional Development Councils (DDCs)

The DDCs began with a flourish. Dr. N.M. Perera in his budget
speech of 1970 introduced them as follows: "An entirely new structure
for planning is being established ...... (within which) each local
authority area will be the focus for development planning and plan
implementation. Popular participation will be secured through Divisional
Development Councils in which the elected organs of the village, the co-
operative society, the cultivation committees, the village council, will
have a planning and co-ordinating role in the over-all development of
their area." The Ministry of Planning and Economic Affairs gave them two
priority objectives, "Organising agricultural, industrial, fisheries and
other infra-structure projects for obtaining the maximum participation of
people in the operation and management of projects and providing the
structure and means for obtaining their participation in planning development work", and, "Bringing about a change in the thinking and attitudes
of people in order to get their active participation in development to
achieve the socialist goals of Government". Other objectives related to
appropriate technology, employment and capital saving. DDCs have,
however, become synonymous with a series of small-scale projects set up
since the early 1970s on funds released directly from the Ministry of
Planning and Economic Affairs with no local mobilisation of financial
resources.

In 1978 the DDC was commonly an advisory board with the Member of
the National State Assembly as Chairman and previously 14 other members
(5 of whom were officials). Management was and is usually in the hands
of a DDC Co-operative Society with an official as Chairman. All DDC projects are set up as co-operatives and many of those employed have paid a
subscription to their co-operative. Others can be directly employed by
the co-operative.

But it is precisely in DDC projects that "participation" has been most
difficult to achieve. The "workers" did not choose the project - which as
a rule were established by direct negotiation between the Members of the
NSA and the MPEA[1] - and the project did not grow out of any existing organisation, Rural Development Society or whatever. The workers were recruited
often, for the better paid jobs at least, as a political favour and naturally
looked, and still look, upon the project as a job which should be exchanged
for a better one wherever possible. Finally, there is in many districts
one Development Officer for every 2 or 3 projects, a system which has not
increased their self-reliance. Yet it was precisely because of this
element of participation that DDC projects were to be distinguished from
other projects, whether run by the Small Industries Department, the
Agricultural Department, the Land Commissioner, the Trade Ministry or
Laksala.[2] (Conversely some very small-scale non-DDC projects are
apparently run by the Rural Development Department and apparently are
founded more solidly on "participation".) Yet, the original faults in
the planning of many projects would not have been so serious if projects
had been made to work by the commitment of the workers, the MP and the
community.

Many of the projects initiated have been strongly criticised for
poor initial choice of product or, for agricultural projects, of area and
for subsequent mismanagement. The over-all programme was criticised
certainly for failing to create significant additional employment and

[1] Ministry of Planning and Economic Affairs.

[2] The government handicraft emporium.

precisely for a surrender of control by the central co-ordinating
Ministry.[1] It is clear that many projects have suffered from a variety
of ills, sometimes due to poor management (not laying in sufficient raw
materials or paying sufficient attention to marketing), sometimes due to
restrictive control of management and e.g. insufficient working capital,
sometimes due to lack of enthusiasm by co-operative members, and, of
course, sometimes to poor project choice. No doubt many projects have
managed to stay alive (but are not "viable") by running down their
initial grant.

In an early analysis of several DDC agricultural projects in Kandy,
G. Pieris commented on the role of the member of the NSA as follows:
"At times he has been able to accelerate decision making, to form a channel
of communication between project personnel and higher authority and ...
to by-pass the local officials and obtain adjustments and concessions to
suit specific project needs." However, "In the farm projects which
have been studied it is the power to influence the selection of project
personnel that most members of the NSA appear to have used most frequently.
In the selection of non-official members to the committees of project
management, political links and loyalties have been the principal criteria."[2]
As Pieris remarks, loyalty of individuals to a political representative
has its virtues and advantages, but tends easily to support corruption.
Furthermore, the identification of a project with a political party inevitably gives all project personnel a very short-term time horizon.

These comments on DDC projects mirror the developments on certain
lands taken over in 1972. Indeed the Electoral Land Reform Co-operatives,

---

[1] See H.N.S. Karunatilleka, "An evaluation of the development
programme under divisional development councils in Sri Lanka", in Sri
Lanka Journal of Social Sciences, June 1978.

[2] G. Pieris, "Agricultural growth through 'decentralisation
and popular participation'", Modern Ceylon Studies, January 1972.

which controlled 170,000 acres in 1975, were operating in a very
similar fashion to DDC agricultural projects. While comprehensive accounts
of the experience of ELRCs are not available they are generally considered
to represent the high (or low) point of the predominance of short-term
factional considerations over technical, economic and often human factors.
Interestingly it is recorded that the majority of the directors of these
ELRCs (seven out of eleven of whom were government nominees) were ex-land
holders, businessmen, lawyers and other professionals.[1] Self-management
was clearly not the intention of these co-operatives.

Rather more general information is available on the development of
the Janawasas which controlled some 50,000 acres in 1975. These
received more political attention from the centre, (perhaps more than they
deserved), often had production plans drawn up for them and were often the
recipients of bank loans. Early stages in five Janawasas were described
in another ARTI publication.[2] The general pattern was for existing workers,
if citizens,[3] to become co-operative members together with a number of
youths selected from nearby areas. All members, and non-citizen labourers,
were generally paid the same set wage with the possibility of some eventual
profit sharing. There is no record that any such profit sharing has ever
taken place.

Each of the five Janawasas had an executive committee. In one
instance no executive committee member was elected by the co-operative
members, in two instances, on the other hand, the majority were elected
by the members. For day-to-day work most Janawasas were following traditional management systems although in one instance permanent work groups

---

[1] ARTI, Agrarian reform and rural development in Sri Lanka, Colombo,
1978.

[2] ARTI, New settlement schemes in Sri Lanka, A.O. Ellman and
D. de S. Ratnaweera, Colombo, 1974.

[3] Non-citizens cannot own land and hence cannot become co-operative
members.

had been formed with elected leaders. In fact, Janawasas did offer
an opportunity for capable plantation workers to reach more responsible
positions. However, the later ARTI account stresses that "the inability
of many of the members to adapt themselves to a new social environment and
to observe the norms of co-operative labour and management resulted in
a high drop-out rate in these Janawasas."[1] The earlier ARTI publication,[2]
however, stressed another problem; the difficulty of integrating earlier,
and older, workers with young, new workers let alone the problem of integrating a group of non-citizens who were co-operative employees and not
members. G. Pieris mentions the same problem of factionalism between co-
operative members and employees. He also mentions that very many co-
operative members believed that eventually the land would be parcelled out
to them individually. No doubt many Janawasa members also hoped this.

The decentralised budget

Begun in 1974, the decentralised budget (DCB) has been an imaginative
attempt to increase participation in the planning of local capital expenditure and in many eyes has met with considerable success. Its magnitude
and provisions have changed somewhat being initially a District allocation
(based on population size and "degree of underdevelopment") and becoming
by 1978 a purely electoral allocation. Expenditure under the DCB reached
Rs. 322 million in 1976, Rs. 300 million in 1977 while Rs. 468 million
was foreseen for 1978.[3]

The purpose of the DCB has been to finance capital works "(a) of a
local nature intended to generate increased production and employment in
the rural sector; and (b) for which no provision has been made in the
votes of any Ministry/Department under itemised works." (Circular, Ministry
of Plan Implementation, 31.1.78) The DCB in 1976 and 1977 covered considerable capital work undertaken by the Territorial Civil Engineering
Organisation, primary school construction and most capital work undertaken

---

[1] ARTI, Agrarian reform ..., op. cit., p. 56.

[2] Ellman and Ratnaweera, op. cit.

[3] Some Rs. 50 million was also going as a grant to local authorities
in 1978 outside the DCB. In 1976 and 1977 such grants were passed through
the DCB.

by Village Committees. It is the primary source of financing for purely
district level projects. The chain leading from project proposal to
implementation begins at many levels, including members of the NSA,
Rural Development Societies, Cultivation Committees, Agricultural
Productivity Committees, (as were) and technical departments. It leads
through the Division and the Assistant Government Agent to the Government
Agent and the Regional Development Division of the Ministry of Plan
Implementation. The role of the latter would seem to be largely formal and
only routine checking of cost estimates has apparently been carried out.
In the final resort the members of the NSA, with (until 1977) the Political
Authority at their head, still make the final choice of projects.

There are certain links in the chain which need further investigation
and perhaps strengthening. For example, the present Government is
seeking to lay greater stress on the Rural Development Societies (RDS)
as a source of proposals. However, these RDS are of very uneven nature
and capacity. Village Committees also have to play an important part in
project execution which they sometimes cannot support. Technical departments can still exercise control, within certain fairly narrow limits, of
the choice of projects.

However, despite certain problems, including the lack of any
rigorous institutional machinery at district level to give an alternative
priority to suggested projects, the DCB has been a welcome innovation.
Participants and observers at district level are confident that more
relevant projects are being selected than earlier; technical departments
are more sensitive than before to popular pressure and the alliance of the
GA and the Political Authority strengthened the degree of co-ordination
and control of technical departments' work. The position has apparently
changed since B.S. Wijeweera wrote in his well-known Administration
Report as GA of Badulla in 1969/70 that "even the decisions of District
Co-ordinating Committees have not teeth. A decision taken by a DCC
even on representations made by the people of the area can be set aside
by the Head of Department" (in Colombo). Furthermore, "with ingenuity
a Head of Department is in a position to transfer funds from one district
to another, from one project in a particular area to another if there is
an anticipation of a shortfall of expenditure."

For the whole island expenditure under the DCB in 1975 and 1976 included between 25 and 30 per cent for irrigation works, a further 30 per cent was generally spent on roads executed by central government agencies while in 1976 around 12 per cent went on local government works, again mainly roads. In 1977 apparently the share of education increased considerably although it was already over 20 per cent in 1976. Education reached some 25 per cent of Matara's expenditure in 1977 and a very similar percentage in Puttalam. The importance of irrigation expenditure naturally varies, it was 23 per cent for Puttalam in 1977, only 5 per cent for Matara and around 8 per cent for Galle.

In some Kachcheries it is felt that a greater share of expenditure could justifiably be devoted to minor irrigation. Many districts have a very clear idea of their future priorities in terms of roads but are less clear as regards irrigation. In addition there were in 1978 certain expenditure cut-off points used by the Irrigation Department, namely Rs. 3,500 per acre benefited in minor irrigation schemes and Rs. 5,000 in major schemes. If a project exceeds this per acre cost it is considered not "feasible" and considerable pressure can be exerted at the District level and in Colombo not to carry it out.

One important point of some interest for the future concerns the means by which money given as a District grant was allocated between electorates. In Colombo district money has sometimes been allocated partly on the basis of population and partly on the basis of paddy acreage, thus diverting more funds to the generally poorer areas. In Puttalam a slight trend towards the opposite effect was observed. Apparently in Trincomalee one electorate out of 3 received an average of 53 per cent over a four year period. No doubt any procedure which pushes funds towards the poorer electorates is most desirable but if that cannot be achieved then per capita allocation seems preferable.

It has been noted that in recent years local government capital allocations (in addition to whatever grants local authorities are given to cover current expenditures) have been funnelled through the DCB. However, given a sometimes hazy frontier between Village Committees' responsi-

bilities and the Highway Department's responsibilities, a weak
Village Committee, unable to argue for its funds, could lead to the
neglect of a whole chunk of road construction. The situation was changed
in 1978 to one of allocating Rs. 200,000[1] per electorate for local
government capital works. However, in the way in which this exercise is
carried out, while the local authority chooses which roads or which
wells to construct, the Local Government Department in effect, through
the forms it sends out, determines the mix of roads, wells, drainage
schemes and buildings. There is very considerable risk that the use of
this control will divert funds from local priorities, i.e. from a well
to a road etc. In addition the local government allocations cannot be
used for productive infrastructure (other than roads) and can certainly
not be used for irrigation.

Criticisms of the DCB system have pursued perhaps three main lines.
The first of these is that money has been spent on too many small
projects, spread about so as to display the maximum "visibility" for
the programme. The next is that demands for expenditure for unproductive
purposes, such as the construction of bus stands, have been too readily
accepted. A third is that projects chosen have been inefficient in economic
terms; in some areas there has perhaps been too much emphasis on electrification projects. However, the maximum limit for expenditure on any
irrigation project has been raised from Rs. 3 to 5 lakhs.[2] This suggests
that many projects are relatively large. In reply to the second point it
would appear that the amount spent on non-income generating projects
has been slight. Furthermore, there often is a strong local demand for
such expenditure.[3] There is no doubt that, in relation to the third

[1] This is only Rs. 1,250 per village, a very low figure.

[2] One lakh is 100,000.

[3] Dr. Wickrema Weerasooria has commented that local communities are
more concerned with DCB expenditure on services than on development projects. On rare occasions when major projects were proposed by an RDS,
"the proposals have not been accompanied by any consideration as to
cost-benefit factors ... when they have proposed rural electrification
schemes we have discovered that such schemes will benefit only a few
families." Paper presented at the joint ILO-ARTEP and ARTI seminar,
op. cit.

point, some DCB funds have been used inefficiently. But it can be argued
that this has often been so even with central government projects. It is
far from clear that the DCB is a greater culprit and many observers at
district level are sure it is not. In addition it is clear that technical
departments have not lost control of expenditure decisions. What seems
necessary now is that some machinery, at AGA level perhaps, should be able
to appraise projects and to present alternatives.

District planning

While both the DDCs and the DCB are very major elements in District
planning, they are not the whole story. An indicator to further development
is given by the World Bank sponsored integrated Rural Development Scheme
for Kurunegala which is being followed up in Matara and Hambantota, Nuwara
Eliya and elsewhere. The Kurunegala scheme is, however, as its authors
point out, not a District plan. It is a series of sectoral investment projects together with some very imaginative suggestions for alternative
programmes in such areas as agricultural extension, credit and water management. As such it can serve as a pilot programme area to test new ideas.
But some of these innovative programmes could prove too expensive for
duplication throughout the island.

The Kurunegala pilot scheme did not involve a great deal of
participation, at least not through the people's elected representatives.
It was not built from the bottom upwards. It is in certain respects
akin to the central government sponsored regional schemes such as the
Mahaweli Development Scheme and the Greater Colombo Economic Commission.

However, the Kurunegala scheme as it has been carried out so far,
demonstrates the potential for District planning, as an exercise which
transcends the scope of the DCB. (And indeed the close involvement
between GA and the Political Authority in the DCB automatically extends
their sphere of influence further than the planning of minor capital
works.) The major lesson of the Kurunegala pilot project should be that
planning capital works is not the totality of District planning and that
other programmes must be brought into consideration.

The District planning exercises are being strengthened by a process
of reviving and stimulating village level institutions within specified

electorates (one each in Kurunegala, Hambantota, Galle and Kalutara).
The basic unit in this process is to be the "Village Development Unit"
and the preparation of village development plans by the RDSs is one major
element. Other elements appear to include the establishment of some
small-scale manufacturing enterprises. However, it is understood that no
funds are available for these programmes, outside, of course, the
electorate provision under the DCB.

Participation

Attempts to foster local level planning in Sri Lanka appear
to have been based far more on administrative decentralisation down to the
electorate level than on popular participation in decision making. This
is shown in particular since (i) although "divisional development councils"
were established, the members of these councils were not popularly elected,
but appointed by the MPs; (ii) although rural institutions such as Rural
Development Societies, Cultivation Committees or local government bodies,
i.e. the elected Village Committees, were invited to make project proposals under the Decentralised Budget, final decision making has remained
with the members of the NSA i.e. at a rather high level of responsibility,
the electorate accounting for about four Village Committees, 160 villages
and 70,000 persons (figures of 1971). Indeed, one major conclusion of
recent trends in decision making seems to be that the introduction of the
Political Authority or of District Ministers has not involved greater
participation at local levels. The representatives' role has been magni-
fied but the relation of the bureaucracy to the people at large, and
particularly to uninfluential groups of them, has not changed. Similarly
the limited impact of voluntary organisations - even of movements of
country-wide importance such as the Sarvodaya Shramadana Movement - on
development policy indicates the weakness of such non-party political
movements in affecting the institutional system of planning and
decision-making.

Evaluation studies[1] suggest that, in spite of their impressive
number, the institutions and departments involved in local level developments

---

[1] See ARTI, *The role of rural organisations in rural development in
Sri Lanka*, Parts 1 and 2, Colombo, 1977.

have been unsuccessful in decentralising decision-making powers to
any directly representative local body and in organising the whole population through participative institutions. This is confirmed by the
extremely rapid rotation in the establishment and abolition of both institutions and programmes, the last examples of which are the cultivation committees and the agricultural productivity committees. Furthermore we
have seen how these bodies were unable to act for the community as a
whole, or for that part of the community they were supposed to help. But
while the creation of any new additional institution at local level should
be strongly opposed, the evolution of some existing organisation into a
local council with real responsibilities is no doubt still possible. The
statement of the Seers report is still valid: "Unless the Government is
prepared to take a deep breath and run the risks of giving true responsibility to local councils, it is hard to see how traditions of responsible
democracy are ever going to be developed in Sri Lanka's countryside, or
how the benefit compliance patterns of government, essentially obstructive
to development, will ever be broken."[1]

In this respect, the current evolution of both the RDSs and of the
VCs may be beneficial. Until 1977 the RDSs, created and run like co-
operatives, had only limited influence at the village level. This
situation may now change although given the extremely rapid setting-up
of one (new) RDS for each village, with 20,000 expected for the end of
1978, the traditions of political, caste, landlord or kinship patronage
in most rural institutions, among which the RDSs have been no exception,
may prevent them from becoming over-all representative and participatory

---

[1] Matching employment opportunities and expectations. A programme
of action for Ceylon, ILO, Geneva 1971, p. 160.

bodies.[1]

On the other hand, the Village Committees have lost a great part of their influence in line with the greater control exercised by MPs especially in the DCB. This was not an illogical outcome of the tentative decentralisation of the budget, since Village Committees appear to have failed in developing their infrastructure for self-management and popular participation, although their financial and decision-making powers have always been very limited. The level of administrative and spatial competence of the Village Committee appeared as intermediate between the population and the district when the electorate was not as important a level as it is now; yet no doubt the Village Committee area was always too big for generating genuine participation at village level. Their loss of command over local development activities is therefore unlikely to imply a big change - in terms of participation - at village level. Such participation requires entities at the real village level, conserving authority and democratic representation of the whole population, together with command over a budget. An appropriate level for a relatively autonomous local decision-making body is probably that at which most RDSs should operate, i.e. the bigger villages.

Any new style local body would have as a major task the elaboration of a programme of local works. For this technical support would be necessary. It is clear that there is a local demand for specific technical support and assistance and hence a local interest in the supply of prompt, skilled and efficient services by technical departments. Some of these, however, are not responding flexibly to the needs of decentralised planning. Parallel to this local responsibility will have to go a certain amount of autonomy in budgetary decisions. Finance for these village level bodies would be partly supplied by the sources which previously were fed into the Village Committees. However, other sources could be envisaged including even a part of the DCB. Controls over such local expenditure

---

[1] A pessimistic view here is presented by G.H. Pieris in his paper, "Local level institutions and participation", presented to the joint ILO/ARTEP and ARTI seminar, op. cit., in which he writes, "Leadership roles in rural institutions provide legitimacy to the power which individuals from the privileged sections of the community already possess."

could require a fixed share of their total expenditure to take
the form of capital projects and for these projects to fall within certain
specified fields. Some programmes could be co-ordinated between villages.
A well-tested village level programme of this nature would be one step
towards achieving local participation and would certainly channel funds
directly from the Centre to the local level.[1]

It has been argued that some earlier reasons for encouraging popular
participation in Sri Lanka are no longer valid. Above all the bureaucracy
can no longer be considered alien and indeed in its values and orientations
it is apparently converging with the group of people's representatives
and office holders. It is probably also generally true, as Pieris claims,
that, "The ideal of a community - a close-knit group of people -
attempting to elevate themselves by a common, communal and selfless effort
seems anachronistic for many parts of the country."[2] Pieris concludes
that under these conditions to expect a high level of popular involvement
in decision-taking would appear unrealistic. It is more than likely that
no advance can be made towards greater popular participation until a
greater consciousness emerges of the differential distribution of the
benefits of government programmes and of conflicting interests within
communities.

---

[1] Above all the need for continual evaluation of any new programme
must be stressed. The absence of monitoring of the activities of e.g.
Cultivation Committees and Agricultural Productivity Committees no doubt
contributed to their collapse.

[2] Pieris, op. cit.

CHAPTER 8
Education and Health Policies

Education policies

We have described at an early stage of this study the level of
resources which Sri Lanka is devoting to education. Given their
importance a separate section dealing with education policies is
justified. We have also noted how enrolment rates vary with household
income level and how, in many cases, children from poor families pass
more slowly through the education system than the children of the rich.
In the first chapter we also saw how enrolment and progression rates in
education had shown no significant improvement for a number of years.
Corresponding somewhat to this situation it can be pointed out that real
public recurrent resources spent on education increased very quickly from
the mid-1950s to the mid-1960s at nearly 5 per cent per annum. From the
mid-1960s to the mid-1970s, however, the rate of increase slowed to a
little over 2 per cent. However, compared to an earlier period considerable
improvements have nonetheless been made. Thus pupil/teacher ratios fell
between 1961 and 1975 from 35:1 to 24:1 for grades 1-8 and from 25:1 to 22:1
for grades 9-12. The capital budget for education has, however, increased
fairly slowly in real terms, at under 2 per cent per annum since the mid-
1950s.

But to appreciate educational policies in Sri Lanka one must see
how education interacts with the labour market. Firstly a disproportionate
amount of years of education is "unemployed". Thus for 1971 it can be
calculated that the unemployed aged 15+ had nearly three years more education than the average for the population of that age. While they amounted
to some 7 per cent of the population in that age group the unemployed claimed
some 10 per cent of its education, measured in years. Thus at any time a
considerable amount of the education generated by the system is being used,
in a socially rather inefficient way, to find work rather than to work.

Correspondingly the employed have become, on average, more
educated than before. Table 1 shows how between 1963 and 1971 the
average amount of education of the employed rose by some 0.6 years,
ranging, however, from 0.1 years for agricultural workers to 1.3 years
for professional and managerial workers. But it is particularly interes-

ting to see in Table 1 that the ratio of years of education of each occupation to the average hardly changed. Thus professional and managerial workers continued to have received some 2-3 times the average amount of years of education and agricultural workers only 70 per cent of the average. The extra years of education cascading onto the labour market have been channelled into various occupations in the same proportions as before.[1]

Table 1: The education of the employed labour force, 1963 and 1971

Occupation	Share of employment		Years of education		Ratio years/ employment	
	1963	1971	1963	1971	1963	1971
Professional and managerial	5.6	5.3	11.0	12.3	2.3	2.3
Clerical	3.8	4.0	9.7	10.6	2.0	2.0
Sales	6.7	7.8	6.1	7.0	1.3	1.3
Production	22.8	26.6	5.1	6.5	1.1	1.2
Services	8.2	5.5	4.8	5.2	1.0	1.0
Agriculture	52.8	50.7	3.5	3.6	0.7	0.7
Total	100	100	4.8	5.4	1.1	1.0

Source: Department of Census and Statistics, Census of Population, 1963 and 1971.

The implication of this is that "educational inflation" is still continuing and can presumably be expected to go further. "Education" can hardly be expected to spill over into the middle grade occupations on any significant scale until the thirst of the higher occupations is satisfied. Conversely the educated themselves are not yet willing to join these other occupations. Educational inflation in professional, managerial, and clerical occupations stems from both demand and supply factors. On the supply side increasing numbers of more highly educated school leavers are chasing relatively few jobs and on the demand side

---

[1] In fact at the level of two decimal places the ratio for agricultural workers in Table 1 fell from 0.73 to 0.67.

employers, above all the public sector, are willing both to see average educational qualifications rise for any occupational group (and also phase out those occupations requiring a lower level of education, e.g. attendants in favour of nurses) and to use educational qualifications as a relatively "neutral" selection procedure. Under these conditions the structure of the education system is itself likely to be perpetuated. Instead of the existence of educated unemployment acting as an incentive to the reduction of secondary education (and thus perhaps providing the conditions for a greater "levelling up" in primary education) the reverse occurs. "O" level passes are first downgraded as job tickets and then "A" level passes. This in its turn leads to further pressure to expand universities and technical colleges.

The role of selection, of course, is by no means diminished in this process so that examinations are of paramount importance. Thus a common curriculum has to be adopted for all schools and those schools which are often unsuccessful in examinations still follow the same curriculum as those which are more successful, and their pupils still leave school without their passes. Suggestions have often been made for separating selection criteria from the daily curriculum so that cramming can be avoided, subjects are taught in a more enjoyable and, one hopes, a more useful way for the early school leaver. But to demand imaginative change from a system which has expanded rapidly and is badly short of complementary materials is probably unrealistic.

However, it has often been stated that the educational system could do more to change attitudes, both of children and of parents. The much-used concept of a "mismatch of opportunities" (i.e. for manual, insecure work) and "aspirations" (i.e. for white-collar, secure jobs) results from an analysis of the education system which shows it holding out the promise of good jobs as an inducement to work hard in school. Correspondingly, the curriculum and examination content used in schools are oriented away from the daily life of the mass of the people. The Seers report[1]

---

[1] ILO, op. cit.

considered "One consequence of this is that the knowledge and skills acquired by the majority who fail the tests (i.e. "O" and "A" levels) ... are inappropriate to their needs and those of the nation. Given also the rigidity of the centralised examination system, they are often inappropriate for those who proceed ... Even more crucial in the long run is the effect on attitudes. The frustration and consequent sense of alienation of those who fail are easily imagined. The effect on the lucky ones who succeed can be, if anything, worse. For many years they have been conditioned to look on learning as a means not of gaining the knowledge to do a job but of gaining the qualifications to get one".

One remedy suggested by Seers was the introduction of pre-vocational courses for grades 6, 7 and 8, (i.e. before the main "O" level course work in grades 9 and 10). "Schools should be transformed (during this period) into centres of rural development, community workshops, centres of craft training and places where the farmer can come to repair his cart ...". Furthermore promotion from grade 8 to grade 9 should depend on aptitude tests, allowing children to give full weight to the practical subjects in grades 6-8. In this way, it was hoped, "O" level failures would at least have followed some more practical and worthwhile courses while those who passed "O" level would have a more rounded view of the world at large.

Pre-vocational studies were introduced in the early 1970s for some 20 per cent of school time in grades 6-9 inclusive. Their main features were described as:

(i) learning a set of carefully selected psychomotor skills directly related to a vocation;

(ii) carrying out manual work geared towards production;

(iii) emphasising the cognitive aspects associated with each vocation;

(iv) changing the affective domain of pupils (e.g. attitudes);

(v) internalising positive values such as dignity of labour, self-discipline, and co-operation.[1]

---

[1] W. Diyasena, Pre-vocational education in Sri Lanka, The UNESCO Press, Paris, 1976.

These aims are not unlike the original intentions of the central
schools set up in 1941, "to correlate the education imparted to the needs
of the locality, to prepare pupils for life and according to their ability
and natural aptitudes; by creating a love for the village environment
and by concentrating on ocupations, traditional or otherwise, which
could be developed nearer the pupils' home ..."[1] But despite the many
advantages of such a prevocational programme there are questions to be
raised concerning this, some 20 per cent, allocation of learning time.
The problem of whether prevocational subjects are to play their part
in selecting the future elite or are to be taught at a level which all
pupils can enjoy has been posed by Dore,[2] "If pre-vocational studies
become an "easy" subject, then they may be taken more seriously than
if they were not examined at all, but not much more seriously. There
will be every reason for making it a difficult subject so that it is taken
seriously. This will mean increasing the complexity of the mathematics
and general science or economics hung on to the peg of the craft activity,
increasing the number of facts to be memorised for reproduction in the
examination, increasing, in short, the third, the general education
elements, of the three elements listed above. And as this happens pre-
vocational studies move further and further away from the craft activity
which is their supposed focus; they become instrumentalised as another
rung on the ladder into the favoured 10 per cent elite; a means of
escaping the necessity of ever having to practise the craft in earnest."
And, one can add, the more the related mental abilities are stressed the
less will the pre-vocational studies' programme change the relationship
of home background variables to educational success.

On the distributional side there are certain comments which can
be made of other suggested innovations. Firstly the Seers' suggestion
of greater reliance on aptitude testing can be criticised. Such testing
requires more imaginative teaching methods in order to be successful

---

[1] J.E. Jayasuriya, Education in Ceylon before and after Independence,
Colombo, 1969, cited in R. Dore, Marga, Vol. 2, No. 2, 1973.

[2] R. Dore, Marga, op. cit.

and, as Blaug has it, "if we are going to abolish examinations and replace
them with aptitude tests, the worst place to start is in the less
developed countries."[1] Secondly, while there are many forms of aptitude
testing, none would appear to be capable of abstracting from home background variables and abilities developed by the school. Indeed results of
aptitude tests would seem to be frequently well correlated with those
of conventional examinations. Shifting to aptitude testing then, if that
were a real possibility, might improve the content of the school curriculum
but it is not at all obvious that it would have beneficial distributional
consequences. Indeed there is a suspicion that in many forms of aptitude
testing the children of the rich would be even more likely to out-perform
the children of the poor.

Given the magnitude of the formal education sector in Sri Lanka
and furthermore given its political prominence as a stake in inter-
linguistic, ethnic and religious group struggles it is perhaps natural that
the power of this sector to bring about social change should have been exaggerated. The Seers report associated the education system with the prevalence of unemployment (via the mechanism of attitude-creation). It could
equally well be asked whether the 1971 insurgency could not have been
averted by earlier educational changes or whether the recent brain-drain
might have been reduced. However, unless a direct link between educational
expansion and low levels of economic growth and job creation can be proved
it is doubtful if the education system can be justly blamed for such phenomena.
No doubt education has raised expectations and aspirations which some people
have left the country to seek. Others, from professional classes, have been
building on the "adaptability" which their Westernised English speaking
background gave them. If the insurgency stemmed in large part from an up-
surge in the impatience of the rural underprivileged then no doubt widespread education had fanned that impatience into flame. But only a repres-
sive educational system with an open denial of equality of opportunity
would not have done so. In short, we consider that the educational system
reacts to social forces and can do very little to change them.

We would not wish, however, to play down totally efforts of e.g.
Sarvadoya and, earlier, Buddhist revivalist movements to inculcate
attitudes of self-reliance and to persuade the educated they have a responsibility to assist in community development. But, in general, where, as
nearly everywhere, the government is taking responsibility for development,
such efforts are inevitably the exception. Correspondingly the rule is that

---

[1] M. Blaug, Education and the Employment Problem in Developing Countries,
ILO, Geneva, 1973.

the educated should assist community development from within the government.

Health policies

As we have discussed in Chapter 1, Sri Lanka has had a good record
in both the achievement of high health standards and the provision of
health services. Life expectancy rose during the 1950s and 1960s from
some 58 years to nearly 66 years. The crude death rate has fallen to
around 8 per mille during the 1970s although it shows little indication
of falling further. Again during the 1950s and 1960s the share of infant
deaths (below one year of age) in all deaths fell from some 26 per cent to
20 per cent and the share of deaths of children aged 1-4 fell from some 20
per cent to 11 per cent. Trends in morbidity cannot be measured although
the number of visits per person to out-patient departments of hospitals
and to government dispensaries and clinics remained at around 3 per person
throughout the 1960s. On the other hand the number of cases treated in
government hospitals has risen faster than the rate of population growth,
but so also has the capacity of the hospitals. According to these "in-
patient" statistics the incidence of diseases of infancy has fallen
sharply while that of anaemia and malnutrition has risen. This may, of
course, be caused by a greater willingness to accept such patients for
treatment.

The general disease pattern in Sri Lanka is marked by a predominance
of respiratory diseases, infective and parasitic diseases and skin diseases. This pattern appears to be fairly stable and, it is generally
assumed, will not vary without major changes in people's daily environment.

Sri Lanka's health services can certainly be commended for their
coverage. The doctor (western-style doctor) population ratio in the
early 1970s was higher than in India or Thailand and the nurse/population
ratio was much the same as in Thailand, and four times higher than in
India. The number of government doctors rose from below 1,000 in 1955 to
some 2,150 where it has stagnated during the 1970s. The number of
hospital beds is currently one per 330 persons and during the 1970s this
ratio was constant. The adequacy of measures of hospital bed availability
is, however, bedevilled by problems of "by-passing". In general, however,
it is probably adequate and many observers consider that in-patients are
sometimes admitted too rapidly. A problem in judging changes in the real

level of health resources through time is that of finding an appropriate price deflator to apply to the trend of health expenditures. Between
the mid-1950s and the mid-1970s these more than tripled in current prices.
However, salaries more than doubled in money terms so that the real
increase in i.e. current expenditures was around 2.4 per cent p.a. and
in capital expenditures somewhat less. During the 1970s the rate of real
expenditures may have fallen off; however, it is more disquieting that
the ratio of doctors and (less qualified) assistant medical practitioners
to total population fell from 1:3,800 in 1971 to 1:4,250 in 1976. This
coupled with drug scarcities and rising costs, must indicate a recent deterioration in levels of medical care.

We have already quoted the statistic from the 1969/70 Socio-economic
Survey that the government sector supplies around 54 per cent of health
care in terms of patient contacts. In terms of expenditure the public
sector in fact supplies somewhat more, around 60 per cent, while other
data suggest a larger role for the non-government sector in out-patient
care. The WHO[1] has presented data suggesting a general average of between
5 and 6 patient contacts (outside hospitals) per person per year of which
some 54 per cent were in the private sector. The WHO data suggest
that private ayurvedic care is 80 per cent of the level of government
western medical care, the socio-economic survey suggested the former
was only one third of the latter. But while there are indeed some 16,000
ayurvedic practitioners, of varying degree of skill and recognition
(and only some 300 are in public employment) a large number only
practise their skills part-time. In any event the potential of this large
and generally relatively cheap source of medical care is hardly exploited.
Integration of Western and traditional medicine is by all accounts far
less developed than in India.[2]

It can fairly be said that the public medical services of Sri Lanka
are well oriented towards caring for the poor. Their distributional impact

---

[1] See on this and many other issues, "Better health for Sri Lanka",
Dr. L.A. Simeonov, WHO, New Delhi 1975.

[2] It is interesting to note that acupuncture treatment by Chinese
trained Sri Lankan doctors is given in a (western-style) Colombo
hospital.

was seen earlier. Objectively the system caters for everyone, but the
rich spend significant amounts per capita in order to use private health
systems. While, however, the issue of distribution of benefits is central
to any assessment of the basic needs impact of a health policy there is
another major issue, namely that of efficiency. It is not a sign of efficiency to be quick in curing the poor of diseases they need never have
caught. Drawing very largely on the Simeonov study[1] a number of issues can
be mentioned. One is the lack of integration of the various health programmes, i.e. public health, major disease control and curative. They
come together neither at the village level nor in any kind of rural health
centre. Another is simply the absence of complementary facilities such as
drugs and transport, which are required for the system to function properly.
A third is the phenomenon of under-utilisation of certain local level units
and the over-utilisation of others, the so-called by-passing. This is
caused by people's certainty that medical care is better in certain institutions, usually those with the greater number of doctors and/or speci-
alists, than in others. However, with a rising scarcity of doctors this
may worsen and institutional controls and some form of zoning would
need to be introduced.

A type of inefficiency which the WHO study hints at is that of
devoting resources disproportionately to curative rather than preventive health activities which, the report estimates, account for only
12 per cent of expenditures. Only in the field of family health, e.g.
surveillance and immunisation, is prevention given more resources than
curing. The relatively small number of public health inspectors, their
restricted training (one year) and the large share of their working time
apparently spent on administration, travel and non-productive activities
(over 75 per cent) together with the general hospital/doctor bias of the
government medical system are all part and parcel of this problem. This
issue of curative versus preventive medicine finds an echo in our data on
morbidity and on water and sanitation facilities. These data suggest a
possible link between the relative incidence of disease and of low quality
facilities.

A similar point can be made in relation to nutrition. Acute and
chronic undernutrition vary considerably between different areas of Sri

---

[1] Dr. L.A. Simeonov, op. cit.

Lanka and in some they are relatively prevalent.[1] Intervention through
nutrition programmes is apparently fairly effective for in-school primary
school children, some 85 per cent of whom received food supplements in
1976. However, as noted elsewhere, the children of the very poor start
school late and drop out early. However, pre-school children are far
less likely to be reached, especially it would appear, in estate areas.
At the end of 1976 only some 200,000 out of around 2 million pre-school
children were receiving food supplements. But according to the nutrition
status survey some 600,000 children (in rural and estate areas) were suf-
fering from chronic undernutrition. Presumably most under-nourished children are either not picked up by surveillance practices or fail to apply
for available food supplements.

A final point to be mentioned concerns the skills used by the
government medical system and their appropriateness in a basic needs
context. Past trends were in favour of phasing out lesser qualified
western-style medical staff and increasing the number of the more highly
qualified, e.g. doctors instead of assistant medical practitioners and
nurses instead of attendants. The number of nurses seems to have held up
fairly well, not so the number of doctors. Access to doctors' time has
to be rationed and more use made of assistant medical practitioners. At
the village level the most frequent government medical representative is
the public health midwife of whom there are some 2,000. Their functions
are obviously limited and are not predominantly curative. There are
only some 100 public health nurses. The government, therefore, has no
village level health worker, hence, presumably to an important extent, the
private use of the obviously widespread (and in many areas competing and
specialised) unqualified or traditionally qualified ayurvedic physicians.
Reports pay lip service to the need to bring some of these people into the
health care delivery system, "particularly in the field of primary health
care."[2]

---

[1] "Sri Lanka nutrition status survey", U.S. Department of Health,
Education and Welfare in co-operation with the Government of Sri Lanka,
CARE and USAID, 1976.

[2] Ministry of Health, Sector Paper, 1978.

The government certainly is not proposing to institute a village level health care worker. Instead community health workers are suggested[1] i.e. educated girls who would assist the public health midwives. In principle this move is welcome and, no doubt, willing applicants would be available. Furthermore community participation in their selection should be encouraged. But there can be no doubt that many people will continue to consider the credentials of the local ayurvedic physician superior in curative matters. The private ayurvedic sector should therefore be involved in selection and possibly supervision of these community health workers.[2]

While community health workers can play an important supporting role in, in particular, mother and child care programmes through undertaking more widespread surveillance and immunisation another kind of local-level worker may also be needed. It has emerged frequently from our discussion that over-all public health and environmental sanitation levels are low despite the existence of over 1000 public health inspectors. Simeonov,[3] found that these inspectors spend no more than 22 per cent of their time on diagnostic, prophylactic and promotional measures. It seems absolutely necessary that a village health worker (perhaps some 20 per public health inspector) should report to the inspector. Together they would survey and draw up proposals on various aspects of environmental sanitation and drinking water needs. Correspondingly a part of the funds allocated to district planning could well be set aside for implementing the proposals of these public health teams. Active involvement of the beneficiary population could easily be built in to such a programme.

The distribution of education and health resources, a comparison

Table 2 puts together a set of data, which no doubt are in certain ways only approximate, on the use of education and health resources by income group and their financing. It is, for example, clear that while

---

[1] Ministry of Health, op. cit.

[2] Nor should one neglect the potential of the 2,500 private sector pharmacists and their assistants in combatting primary health care problems.

[3] Dr. L.A. Simeonov, op. cit.

only the richest 2 per cent spend more on education than the government
spends for them the richest 20 per cent spend more on health than the
government spends for them. Total expenditure, public and private, by
the richest group on health is less than double that of the poorest,
for education it is five times as much. Health and education systems in
this respect obey very different laws. There is a sense in which an
expenditure of some Rs. 8.0 for health per person would be "adequate" since
that represents the level of resources consumed by those who have the
power to choose. Education on the other hand is so strongly related
to competition for scarce jobs that a similar level for "adequacy" based
on the expenditure levels of the rich could never be decided. To fix
a target of that nature is chimerical.

To reach a per capita expenditure of Rs. 8.0 for health, keeping
personal expenditures unchanged, would have required per capita public
expenditure to rise from Rs. 3.30 to Rs. 5.50 (66 per cent). To reach
average per capita expenditures in education for those below the average
of Rs. 12.10, keeping private expenditure constant would require an additional government expenditure of Rs. 1.76 per person. On this basis
additional expenditures might be more usefully devoted to health than
to education.

However, it may well be when discussing the case of extra funds
in health and education systems that additional expenditure need not
be the best way to raise health standards. In any event there are other
objections to this approach. In health additional government expenditure would, judging by the 1973 distributional pattern, stand a good
chance of being used to benefit the poor. In education the chances
are slight. Secondly, achieving an improved education coverage is far
more a question of re-orienting resources than of expanding them, although
school wastage should be lessened if more books or forms of financial
assistance were available. The minor point is that private expenditures
in health will probably never be eliminated since in this personal and
sensitive area people will always insist on making their own choice
outside the publicly offered services. The arguments do, however, strongly
suggest one thing, namely that health should in general have priority for

Table 2: Expenditures on health and education, 1973, Rs. 2 months

Income group per cent	Private		Government		Total	
	Health	Education	Health	Education	Health	Education
6.9	1.3	0.8	4.8	6.1	6.1	6.9
27.3	1.5	1.1	4.0	7.2	5.5	8.3
45.5	2.1	2.4	3.2	8.9	5.3	11.3
16.7	3.4	5.6	2.5	11.0	5.9	16.6
1.6	6.2	9.8	1.9	11.7	8.1	21.5
2.0	9.8	21.4	1.2	12.7	11.0	34.1
Average	2.5	3.3	3.3	8.8	5.8	12.1

Source: P. Alailima, op. cit., Central Bank of Ceylon, Survey of Ceylon's Consumer Finance, 1973.

funds over education. It is apparent from the private expenditure
figures that the poor simply appear to consider health, or, one should
say, increments to publicly supplied levels of health care, more
important to them than education.

There are two steps we would like to suggest at this stage in order
to bring about a more equitable distribution of public resources for
education and health.

In education we would like to recommend a serious background study to be
undertaken under the aegis of the Ministry of Education. This would require
test scores relating to different kinds of mental abilities for children at
different age and grade levels. These test scores, and changes in these
test scores between different ages and grades, should be analysed in relation
to home background factors, e.g. parental education, occupation, reading
materials in the home etc., and to in-school factors, e.g. regularity of
school attendance, teacher training etc. The objective of such an exercise
would be, firstly, to pin-point certain remedial needs and, secondly, to
publicise and to concentrate attention on differential school achievement
between various groups and areas. There is also a need to take a serious
look at the prevocational programme in order to analyse the many ramifications
of the system both in relation to past performance and in relation to future
requirements.

In the field of health care we would suggest firstly greater use of
income or occupation as an indicator of target groups for special programmes.
Nutrition programmes, for example, are targetted at all mothers and children
picked up by screening, clinic visits etc. It is, however, well established
that nutrition problems are more severe for the poor and most of the poorer
groups are in rural areas. One means of action might be a conscious policy
of siting clinics, or conducting mobile sessions, in poorer villages or,
frequently, in the newly expanded hamlets and dependencies of existing
villages, such as encroacher communities. As a long term suggestion we would
like to stress the need for evolving a regular mechanism for policy co-
ordination in the fields of food, nutrition and agricultural development.

CHAPTER 9

Summary and Conclusions

Introduction

In this chapter we shall first summarise the main points of the preceding chapters. This will complete our first objective of Chapter 1, namely to review the over-all state of basic needs satisfactio. We shall then draw certain conclusions on the role of welfare policies in the economy of Sri Lanka. These conclusions will refer back to the second and third objectives of this study that we discussed in Chapter 1. They concern the effects of welfare policies on economic growth and on the social structure.

Summary

In Part I (Chapter 2) we examined some very broad indicators of basic needs satisfaction and began by comparing these indicators for Sri Lanka with those for other countries. There we noted the country's high relative score in many areas including that of per capita calorie consumption. This last, we also mentioned, is associated with the high share of food imported. We saw that some of these relatively high levels of basic needs satisfaction either date back for a number of years or are the result of trends, e.g. in death rates, which began fifty years back. For education and health care we looked at total public and private resources used up. In comparison to many other developing countries the over-all resources committed are not always so high, however, the government share of these resources is relatively high. We also drew attention to two less satisfactory indicators, one is the lack of improvement in educational enrolment in recent years and the other is the over-all position as regards water and toilet facilities.

We continued the discussion by a disaggregation first to district level and then to income group. The district level analysis showed a noticeable but not always uniform spread. Clearly districts with a significant estate population fare badly on infant mortality, female life expectancy and infant malnutrition. Conversely the districts close to Colombo score well on most indicators and in remoter rural areas while education indicators may be low health indicators are generally at the national average.

Turning to the cross-classification by income group we found that income effects were greatest in those sectors where official programmes

are least developed, i.e. housing space, sanitary facilities and adequacy
of water sources (quality and quantity). Income effects are, however,
influential in all basic needs areas in determining the access of the poor.
Calorie consumption is less than proportionate for about the poorest 40
per cent of the rural population. It may be absolutely insufficient
for the same group. Education enrolment rates rise with income and, furthermore, even among in-school children the offspring of the rich are more successful. Morbidity would seem to be highest in rural areas and for the poorest
income groups on estates. We conclude therefore that while Sri Lanka has
been successful in taking the distribution of certain welfare inputs out
of the hands of the market and setting up a more egalitarian allocation
system, there are still contradictions. The level of health is affected
not only by a fair distribution of health care facilities but also by an
income determined distribution of drinking water, housing and sanitary
facilities. Education is far more widely spread than in many countries.
But income becomes the more important in determining educational levels
the more these help in the job search. And, of course, there are home
background factors whose effects on educational outcomes can only be minimised and never suppressed.

In Part II (Chapters 3 and 4) we shifted our focus to certain factors
relating to income distribution and poverty. We began by revising household
survey data on over-all income distribution both by taking account of household size and of possible varying levels of underestimation of different
income sources. These revisions revealed the dependency of poor households
on labour incomes. We also studied certain more detailed data on income
sources. This revealed, for example in rural areas, that "cereal" income
by no means accrues more than proportionately to the poor. We examined two
broad sets of trend data; the first relates to consumer prices, manufacturing
output prices and producer rice prices. This showed the internal barter terms
of trade favouring agriculture in the late 1960s and early 1970s, but not
later. This was largely caused by changes in the food subsidy system (in
the late 1960s) and poor harvests (early 1970s). Nevertheless domestic
paddy prices have been below import prices since the mid-1960s. The other
set of data relates to wage differentials. Over a long period differentials
between rural labour and organised urban labour have probably increased
although those between rural labour and professional groups have fallen.

Chapter 4 looks specifically at poverty, concentrating on low
income groups. It points out that diversity of income sources is less
common for the poor than the non-poor so that one source of income cannot

compensate for a fall in the other. In rural areas poor "employees" are
more likely to be found in agriculture than in industry, with the exception
of food, beverages and tobacco manufacturing. The chapter also reviews
weekly hours worked, and finds that for labourers earnings hardly fall
with hours worked, and the phenomenon of unemployment. Here we find
that, in terms of earnings foregone, unemployment hurts the poor more
than other groups. We finally look at the particular conditions of rural
wage labour and of estate labour and of the expansion of small-holder
cultivation onto marginal land. For rural wage labour we note both the
diversity of their backgrounds (and therefore possibly of their interests)
and their similarity in income and economic terms to certain forms of
tenancy. For estate labour we note the failure of remedial legislation
to ensure their achievement of reasonable levels of basic needs satisfaction. We finally note some drawbacks of the programme of village
expansion and the particular problems associated with increased population
density in rainfed farming in the Dry Zone.

In Part III (Chapter 5) we looked at some major structural features of
the economy of Sri Lanka. These included the diminishing size of paddy land
holdings which have fallen from some 2.2. acres on average in 1946
to less than 1.5 today. We discussed the pre-land reform position of the
estates and their general tendency not to build up replanting reserves.
Outside agriculture we noted the much increased share of manufacturing
in GNP but found nonetheless that the over-all structure of employment
is by no means changing in the direction of providing more secure jobs.
We discussed the breakdown of employment and value-added by major employer
noting that the public sector accounts for 40 per cent of non-agricultural
employment. Finally we looked at the land reform exercise which was
carried out in two rounds in 1972 and 1975 and suggested that it left
the average private (non-public company owned) estate with around 70-80
acres. The land reform brought some two-thirds of the total tea area but
only one-third of the total rubber area into government hands. Land taken
over was subsequently managed through a variety of institutional forms
and only a minor part, and that usually of low quality land, was distributed
for individual cultivation.

In Part IV (Chapters 6, 7 and 8) we looked at selected policy areas.
Chapter 6 concentrated on rural policies. It discussed first the over-all
tenancy situation in Sri Lanka and the policy steps taken to control rent
levels and provide security of tenure. These have generally failed and may

have even aggravated the insecurity of tenants. We then discussed the
guaranteed price scheme and the categories of farmers likely to benefit from
it. Clearly these are only the larger surplus producers. A similar situation
applies in relation to the provision and use of various inputs, e.g. credit,
fertilizers and pesticides. In many cases larger farmers with secure irrigation sources make by far the greatest use of these inputs. Tenant farmers
frequently use little institutional credit as their inputs are supplied by
their landlords, often at high rates of interest. Cultivators of very small
plots are, in any event, less likely to use fertilizer or take institutional
credit. We finally discuss the colonisation and major irrigation programme.
This has accounted for considerable population movement but at a high cost.
Furthermore many "second-generation" problems of (illegal) land mortgaging
and youth unemployment are emerging.

Chapter 7 discusses the nexus of participation, administration and
representation. In Sri Lanka the system of political representation has
been **vigorous** and led to frequent democratic changes of government. In
recent years political representation has increasingly infiltrated into
traditionally adminstrative matters, helped by the decentralisation of
certain levels of decision taking. This has been a hallmark of the
Divisional Development Council programme and of the decentralised budget.
Local level participatory bodies, including village committees, co-
operative societies and rural development societies, are all to a greater
or lesser extent stepping stones and power bases for party politicians.
These institutions are often seen as a means for the more influential
village families to legitimise their power. Meanwhile, however, decisions
on local works and services are being taken at a level which permits
greater interaction of the bureaucracy and the beneficiaries.

Chapter 8 discusses a few issues relating specifically to education
and health policies. It notes the continuation of "educational inflation"
with no apparent brake on the growth of educational requirements for
white collar jobs. The chapter also expresses doubt on the capacity of
a pre-vocational studies curriculum to reduce the effects of home background factors on educational achievement. On the health side the chapter
notes a very probable recent deterioration in the level of health care
provided. It draws attention to the absence of a focal village health
worker and suggests that far greater use could be made of community workers
and of the ayurvedic sector.

Conclusions

Our task in this section is to refer back to the second and third
objectives we specified in the Introduction[1] to this study and, in the
light of the preceding discussion, to answer the questions we raised. These
concerned firstly the possible negative effects of welfare policies on
growth and secondly the interaction of welfare policies and the country's
originally conservative social structure.

We must begin, however, by stressing that Sri Lanka has not been the
model example of the application of a basic needs strategy. Its successes
have been in ensuring a relatively equal distribution of many goods and
services. To that extent its Governments and administration must be con-
gratulated. But it has failed to develop production in line with distribution. Over-all growth has been slow and insufficient jobs have been
created. Furthermore the country has not managed to guarantee the access
of the poor to productive assets and, as we have seen, to that extent
rural policies and land reform have been relatively unsuccessful. Indeed
in some ways the country can be characterised as having provided a minimum
level of basic needs and as ignoring the dynamic elements of the strategy.
However, the sturdiness of parliamentary democracy in Sri Lanka and its
genuine efforts towards encouraging local participation in many fields mark
the country out as something more than an efficient system of rationing.

But the thrust of our first objective is to question whether the
"ideal" basic needs strategy of fair distribution and economic growth was,
and is, realistic for Sri Lanka. It can be asked simply whether the prospects for economic growth were not substantially diminished by the operation
of welfare and subsidy policies. There are a number of points to be discussed here, all of which are also probably relevant for countries similarly
attempting to implement basic needs strategies. These concern the diversion
of public funds from investment to consumption, the disincentive effects of
welfare and subsidy policies and, conversely, their incentive effects, the
viability of such policies in current circumstances and their over-all
effects on attitudes of self-reliance.

---

[1] Our first objective was to review the over-all level of basic
needs satisfaction. This was achieved in Part I.

One simple point of departure is the World Bank's calculation[1]
that had expenditures on welfare programmes and consumer subsidies been
halved from 1945 on and the additional funds invested then, by 1975, per
capita incomes might have risen at some 2.5 per cent p.a. instead of 1 per
cent. Per capita income in 1975 might have been around $200 instead of
$130. As the World Bank paper states, "There is room for disagreement on
the trade-off between a per capita income, of say, 35-55 per cent higher
over 30 years and a worsening, of unknown extent, in life expectancy, infant mortality, literacy and fertility ... . There is little room for
disagreement though on whether (political factors aside) social accomplish-
ments could not have been achieved at a lower cost, such as through a more
selective ration program. This would have allowed maintenance of social
objectives and increased growth."

The World Bank paper does not discuss whether faster growth might have
been accompanied by increased income inequality. What sort of additional
investments were likely? Could there not have been investments made which
would have perhaps achieved growth and equity? Such growth plus equity
yielding investments no doubt are possible to find. They would need to be
concentrated on the assets used and owned by marginal farmers and the landless. Clearly under normal circumstances there are few such assets and
few such investment opportunities. In fact following land reform and co-
operative management of certain estates rather more investment opportunities
present themselves. But this was not so in the 1950s, when public investment was concentrated on large-scale projects particularly in major irrigation schemes (as we noted in Chapter 5). We have reviewed the immediate
distribution effects of large-scale irrigation and land development projects in Chapter 6 and noted their tendency to intensify certain income
inequalities. Faster growth stimulated by such investments might very well
have worsened income distribution.

But even if distributional losses were accepted could not the poor
still benefit through a "trickle-down" process of sharing the fruits of

---

[1] "The relationship of basic needs to growth, income distribution and
employment: the case of Sri Lanka", World Bank, Policy Planning and Program
Review Department. The paper uses a simple incremental capital-output
ratio to calculate this result, assuming a switch of 4.5 per cent of GDP
from consumption to investment.

growth? Here we can only say that if, at least over a 15-year period
the poorest 20 per cent of families saw their share of total income fall from
8 per cent to 6 per cent, they would gain nothing from an over-all growth
rate of 2 per cent. At higher growth rates there would be some absolute
income gains. But it would be precisely this poorest group which under
a different system would have to pay more for its cereal consumption if not
for its use of health and education facilities.

The World Bank paper stresses linkages between basic needs such that
growth might at least indirectly be stimulated. It mentions the probable
effects of literacy on lower fertility rates and population growth, both
directly and by reducing infant mortality.[1] It also states, "Another
apparent reason for low fertility has been the ration (and food subsidy)
and health programs which have lowered the old-age and disability insurance
motivation for having large families."[2]

However, a slightly more pessimistic view is to stress that health
and education may well make their major contribution in improvements in
managing owned or rented assets and at working better at an assured job.
Thus for the landless, jobseeking category better health and education cannot be put to such productive use despite possible benefits in relation to
the adoption of family planning. But this view is too negative. The impact
of the food subsidy has been no doubt partly to contribute to better health.
It has also guaranteed a certain level of security and as such has probably
promoted risk-taking. In certain contexts risk-taking again brings us
back to asset ownership and e.g. readiness to introduce new techniques.
However, in this context risk-taking also covers willingness to attempt
dry-zone cultivation and outside irrigation schemes. This form of cultivation has had considerable benefits (probably not least in reducing rural-
urban migration) and has made use of otherwise valueless assets. It may
thus represent one means by which state-provided "seed capital" has led the
way to output increases.

There are, however, other linkages between welfare and subsidy policies,
on the one hand, and growth, on the other, which should be followed up. The

---

[1] Interestingly the paper remarks in a footnote that education may not
have to be "relevant" to development to have a positive effect on it and
that students manage to acquire useful learning skills in spite of irrelevant
curricula.

[2] World Bank, op. cit.

high share of public health and education expenditure as well as the operation of the net food subsidy suggests that private levels of expenditure
of these items may be relatively low. Thus indeed, we saw in Chapter 2,
Table 2, that private levels of expenditure on health and education in
Sri Lanka are relatively low, below indeed those of India. This again
suggests that private consumption patterns have been oriented elsewhere,
presumably away from agricultural products and towards manufactures. It
is interesting to recall here, that whatever might be said about Sri
Lanka's over-all growth performances, output of manufactures has grown
fast, at very nearly 7 per cent p.a. (in real terms) from 1963-1977. In
India a slow-down in manufacturing growth (from 7 per cent p.a. in the
early 1960s to some 4 per cent in the early 1970s) has been blamed on a
faster rise of food grain prices than of manufactures.[1] Perhaps in Sri
Lanka the opposite has applied.

On the wages side cheap food should in principle have led to low
labour costs and a faster rate of labour absorption. This increase would
be all the greater if there was a sizeable effort in exporting manufactured
products but, as these are customarily understood,[2] this has been lacking
in Sri Lanka. Furthermore, we have noticed, see Chapter 3, that urban labour, at least in the formal sector, has enjoyed a relatively strong bargaining
and real wage position. To that extent food subsidies may not in fact have
lowered wages costs. However, there is no doubt that our earnings data
refer mainly to the more organised parts of manufacturing employment. The
situation in e.g. rural industries may be different.

Two allegedly negative linkage effects can also be reviewed. They
concern firstly the relation of food subsidies to food production and
secondly the relation of welfare programmes to unemployment. Our text
should be sufficient to reduce the suspicion of a disincentive effect on
cereal production considerably. We have shown that surplus farmers receive
a large number of incentives towards increasing output which should well

---

[1] A. Mitra, Terms of Trade and Class Relations, London 1977.

[2] i.e. some "manufacturing" is incorporated in tea and rubber
exports but market conditions are such that no benefits specifically
result from the low labour costs involved.

outweigh any possible disincentive. Poorer farmers would no doubt prefer
a diet composed more of rice and less of cassava if they could manage it.
In general, however, there are a large number of obstacles to increasing
the output of cereals from very smallholdings. Credit, timely inputs,
water control and the small size of holdings themselves are all important.
We doubt if the distribution of free rice is as important as any of these.

The relation between welfare programmes and subsidies and unemployment
is less clear cut. The World Bank paper[1] stresses a number of possible
reasons for high levels of unemployment. One is "voluntary" unemployment.
"If, for example, a government white collar job offers lifetime income,
security, status and career prospects ... then it may be considered worthwhile to wait for that job even if one's chances are only one in three or
four." Another reason is the degree of selectivity with which educated
women may view job opportunities. "...whose parents ... would set limits
as to what kinds of jobs, geographic areas, or residential arrangements
were acceptable." A third reason is that food subsidies (and now income
maintenance for the unemployed) do reduce the costs of waiting and increase
the willingness of relatives to support unemployed members. There can be
no gainsaying this last and more general point. However, in Chapter 4
we tried to put the phenomenon of unemployment into a poverty context and
concluded that it hits the poor most severely. Unemployed members of
poorer households are also the least educationally qualified of all the
unemployed, and the youngest. We doubt, therefore, if "voluntariness"
of unemployment or selectivity in accepting jobs are important for this
group. We would not, therefore, wish to stress possible links between
welfare programmes and the attitudes of the unemployed. However, if welfare and subsidy programmes have been associated with generally low growth
rates then they carry some blame for unemployment among the poor and the
rich.

To single out welfare and subsidy policies as a major contributor to
low rates of economic growth certainly seems problematical. The World
Bank paper[2] justly mentions other reasons for slow growth many of which we

---

[1] World Bank, op. cit.

[2] World Bank, op. cit.

discussed in Chapter 1 or Chapter 5. It wrote, "Unlike the fast growing
East Asian countries, but like India, Sri Lanka has had a Fabian ambivalence
towards the private sector; an over-emphasis on direct controls in place
of price signals and on import-substitution rather than exports; serious
problems with labour management relations; serious administrative and institutional inefficiencies; and active competition between parties for votes,
based to a substantial extent on populist programs and on patronage. In
addition (it had) the burden of having almost 30 per cent of GDP in 1960
in export crops which were to experience a devastating secular decline in
prices over the next fifteen years."

We can look at these reasons for slow growth in more detail. Furthermore we can ask, to the extent that these reasons represent deliberate policy
choice, whether they were themselves the outcome of   compromise between
different group interests or whether they were genuine misapplications of
planning theory. The first reason, ambivalence towards the private sector,
we have discussed in Chapter 5 in relation to estates. The possibility of
nationalisation would clearly seem to have slowed down the rate of investment in the estate sector and probably discouraged it from developing substitutes to the old staples of tea, rubber and coconut. Export diversification
was thus slowed down. However, ambivalence towards the private estate
sector was a deliberate policy choice fostered by the multi-class nature of
the ruling parties. Poor labour-management relations are then simply the
other side of the coin of ambivalent support to both employers and unions.
However, it is doubtful if problems of labour-management relations were a
serious impediment to growth, with one qualification. That is that poor
labour-management relations discouraged private foreign investment (despite
some mutually beneficial counter-examples). But again, Governments were
ambivalent in their attitudes towards private foreign investment anyway.

The mention of emphasis on direct controls rather than price signals
relates mainly to external trade. (Internally price signals were used,
infelicitously, to lower the cost of capital, probably at the expense of
new employment.)[1] The official exchange rate remained unchanged from 1948
until 1977 although a surcharge (FEECs) was applied from 1967 to many imports.
It was not, however, allowed as a bonus to the majority of exports. Trade

---

[1] Combine harvesters were being used to harvest rice in Gal Oya in
the mid-1950s.

policy, both in this respect and in the import-substitution versus exports issue, no doubt has been a drag on Sri Lanka's growth performance. The system of controls, particularly as it was in use in the early 1970s no doubt was inferior as an allocative mechanism to greater use of the price mechanism. The Seers report[1] commented, "We examined procedures for selecting projects to be allocated foreign exchange for imports. Licensing of industrial raw materials determines priority by 'essentiality', of which the only available quantitative indicator seems to be workforce at the factory per dollar applied for. This is a good first approximation to priority but apparently not much attention is paid to the amount or type of extra output expected. This leads to such results as classifying imports of tobacco for local cigarette manufacture as essential." No doubt one reason for preferring controls to the use of the price mechanism, despite it would appear insufficient resources to apply controls well, was the desire to avoid inflation. However, the result was frequently disruption and shortage so that it is doubtful if even any political gain resulted.

The import substitution versus exports issue has a number of ramifications. The foreign exchange scarcity resulting from decreased estate crop earnings led to the encouragement of all kinds of import substituting industries. The profits from import substitution were a disincentive to private exporters of manufactures.[2] Furthermore in the early 1970s the CRA (convertible rupee account) scheme encouraged potential exporters to concentrate on precious stones. In addition a conviction that the State should play a major role in industrial production led to the growth of public sector industry we noted in Chapter 5. Public sector industries immediately risk becoming political playthings both for their price policies and for their job creation potential. They are rarely suited to spearhead an export drive. However, again it is hard to accept that there might be greater political gains from import substitution than from exporting and we would regard trade policy as working against economic growth but not necessarily in favour of any other objective.

The World Bank paper's mention of administrative and institutional inefficiencies draws attention to such matters as the implementation of controls

---

[1] *Matching employment opportunities and expectations, op. cit.*

[2] G. Pyatt et al., *op. cit.* calculated that there was a widespread tax and tariff bias against exporting in the early 1970s. This applied even in sectors such as textiles, rubber products and ceramics where otherwise the possibilities for export were good.

(as we have discussed) and to the implementation of various support programmes for agriculture, such as credit, fertilizer supply etc. Most of
these we have discussed in Chapter 6. It is very doubtful, however, if Sri
Lanka's experience in this area was worse than that of most developing
countries. However, we would like to draw attention to the repeated intention to upgrade coconut production through various support programmes,
without, however, any great action on the ground.

The mention of "populist programmes and patronage" is a general point
which is inherent in much of our account of Sri Lanka. It ties in with
G. Myrdal's criticism of soft states and the absence of compulsion. It no
doubt has significant negative effects on the efficiency of implementation
of many programmes and projects. However, it describes the basic problem,
not a consequence of the problem.

The decline in foreign exchange earnings must naturally be seen as a
crucial element in Sri Lanka's slow growth. If prices had not declined
then the country would now be better off, in many ways. But it is the
Governments' reactions to the decline which are more the issue. These
reactions were so often defensive and inward-looking. Crop diversification
from existing estates was hardly encouraged, as we have noted above, nor
was any successful drive to export manufactured goods undertaken. Certainly
other foreign exchange earnings, such as precious stones and tourism, have
helped the balance of payments. Nevertheless we feel that no Government
had a consistent response to this problem. It can be argued that since
this was the major problem the only possible useful responses would have
been so radical as to upset one major interest group or another. These
responses might have been either a whole-hearted reliance on foreign private
investment leading to export-led growth and/or radical reform of domestic
agriculture in order to give the rural poor directly what a prosperous
estate sector might have given them indirectly. But neither approach was
seriously tried.

We would like to add one more reason for slow growth to the list made
out by the World Bank. This was the country's inability to channel investments to areas which could have used them most productively. We have in
mind small-scale industries which suffered more from exchange control and
the licensing of imports of raw materials than did large-scale industries
and certain parts of domestic agriculture. Even within the paddy sector
attention was focussed on new areas and major schemes. The improvement of
water control in the wet zone, for example, was given far less attention.

Similarly investment in neglected coconut and rubber estates with a planned
programme of more intensive land use would have almost certainly given a
good return on investment. We would consider that the major reasons for
investment being concentrated where it was and for other sectors being
neglected were political. Particularly in domestic agriculture such investments needed prior institutional change before they could be effective.
And this was not forthcoming.

From this very brief review of reasons for slow economic growth in the
Sri Lankan economy we can conclude that most, but not all, were related
to the nature of society and its various interest groups. Some reasons,
however, we felt were not related to any such "political" benefits and could
have been changed without serious political loss. Most of the reasons
nonetheless have their background in the kind of state where various
interest groups are on the whole well-balanced and compromise becomes second
nature. In this light we should look at another possible "negative linkage"
between welfare and growth; namely that such policies actively worked
against creating a climate of self-reliance and instead intensified dependency, an attitude inimical to development. Clearly it is true that in
many instances Sri Lanka Governments have been unable to use compulsion
and to enforce discipline. The very widespread misuse of irrigation water
is the obvious example that springs to mind and, as we noted in Chapter 1,
parliamentary representatives have often played the role of legitimising
such "indiscipline". But in this context welfare and subsidy programmes
are reflecting other forces which themselves no doubt contributed to the
array of reasons for slow growth given above.

There is one more point which should be mentioned at this stage. Sri
Lanka's welfare and subsidy policies have endured for many years, has not
the world changed in ways which will make their continuation more difficult? In many respects the answer is probably no. Many of the inputs
for these programmes consist of semi-skilled labour which the country has
in abundance. However, other inputs are imported and here certain problems
arise. Foreign drugs, for example, are probably far more expensive now in
terms of real local resources than they were. The prices of imported cereals,
however, rise and fall. But the main problem is no doubt the growing gap
in standards of living between Sri Lanka and many other groups of countries.
The result is a "brain-drain" at many levels. Welfare programmes will therefore be forced to change their character and shift to greater reliance on
less-marketable skills. We have mentioned some possibilities for changing

the skill mix in health programmes in the previous chapter.

So far in these conclusions we have mainly discussed our second objective, the relation of welfare state policies to growth. Our general conclusion must be that the negative effects of such policies on growth can easily be exaggerated. Furthermore those policies also have positive effects which are not generally specified. However, any discussion of the interaction of welfare policies and growth must necessarily be country-specific in the sense that one must investigate both what alternative investments were foregone and what was the general social and political climate of the country. For Sri Lanka we are not optimistic that with greater investment resources at hand they would have been fruitfully spent. Correspondingly we feel that the operation of welfare programmes was a reflection of the over-all social and political situation in Sri Lanka and not an aberration from it. It follows that outside attempts to create faster growth in Sri Lanka over the past twenty years were misdirected if they aimed simply at reducing levels of welfare expenditures. It would have been more fruitful to point out firstly means of streamlining welfare programmes and raising their efficiency in terms of their own objectives and secondly means of improving the economic administration of the economy, especially in substituting export-led growth for import substitution.

The third objective we mentioned was to review the interaction of welfare measures with the country's originally very conservative social structure. In Chapter 1 we pointed out some of the ethnic, class, caste and religious differences in the country. In Chapter 4 we stressed the very dependent role of rural labourers, in Chapter 5 the limitations of land reform carried out and in Chapter 6 we discussed the extent of tenancy and the failure of legislation to give security of tenure or fix rents. These are clearly ways in which "traditional" relations have been allowed to endure and reflect Gold's "unresolved compromise"[1] which we mentioned in Chapter 1. The modern, reforming sector (which stresses contractual relationships and job security) has been unable to overcome the traditional sector (which stresses patron-client relations and a multiplicity of personal relationships between worker and land-owner through jobs, credit and rent).

However, the relationship of the two sectors is not simply one of reform versus tradition. The traditional sector in addition produces the food and

---

[1] M.E. Gold, op. cit.

the modern sector consumes it. There is a conflict of interest between the
two which is partly the ubiquitous relation between food producers and consumers. But this conflict is also present within the village. In the
Sri Lankan context the conflict takes an additional form, between the town,
which exports and controls access to foreign resources, and the village
whose interests (or rather the interests of whose leaders) prefer local
production. This suggest that the estates are part of the town, which
owns them, decides what they shall produce and who will manage them, and
not the village. Thus problems of so-called estate-village relations
are far more problems of town-village relations and of different management
and ownership systems.

That the urban-modern sector controls foreign trade has allowed it to
provide cheap food through imports. But in order to placate the traditional
leadership formed by food surplus farmers and for the sake of harmony in
relations between the modern and traditional sector everything has been
done to subsidise farm inputs of seeds, machinery, water and credit. The
subsidies benefited farmers with controlled irrigation who could make good
use of fertilizer, and larger farmers, who could afford machinery. Credit
programmes rose and fell as defaults increased and loans were written off.

However, while support policies have benefited larger farmers and
while these have also been threatened very little by land reform, rent
control or minimum wage legislation other elements of rural society have
gained much less. A large part especially of the rural and "traditional"
population gains nothing but its cheap food. It pays high land rents and
receives very little help and support for the few crops it grows. Above
all it finds insufficient work. No doubt funds invested in the right place
could provide jobs for the poor. The estate takeover may specifically have
opened up these possibilities. But a diversion of funds from food subsidies
to major investment programmes twenty years back would have risked producing an equally inegalitarian rural structure where the rural poor had no
part at all in the compromise between modern and traditional sectors, and
surplus food producers received both subsidised inputs and higher output
prices.

We therefore feel that one effect of the system of food subsidies in
Sri Lanka has been precisely to perpetuate the structure of traditional
relations, particularly in rural areas.[1] Thus Gold's "unresolved compromise" should have a third party added, namely reformers, traditional leader-

---

[1] And possibly for domestic servants in all areas.

ship and traditional followers. But the last group, while numerous, has
gained least. Nor probably have they gained very much from the expansion
of education programmes where clearly household income still has a significant effect on enrolment and progression.

This virtual exclusion of the rural poor from the benefits of the
system of compromise under which Sri Lanka has been ruled for some years is
clearly both unfortunate and dangerous. One might hazard a guess that it
was partly the tradition of caste hierarchy and respect (as well as the
extent of subsidised food programmes) which has allowed the situation to
continue. There are, in principle, two means of changing the current
position of the rural poor (which have already been touched on above in the
context of economic growth; they could also be pursued simultaneously).
One is through the application of radical land reform policies, particularly aiming at some form of collective production. The other is through
the achievement of very fast rates of output growth and consequent "modernisation" of traditional relations. The first was tried, although perhaps
without convincing enthusiasm, in the early 1970s. There was far from total
commitment, the over-all economic and climatic situation was unlucky and
the experiment failed. Currently it seems that the second line is being
followed. Modern sector growth is being aimed for, plus the development of
major irrigation schemes but without interfering with relations within the
traditional sector. Despite its popularity the Government either feels no
need to take such steps or is unwilling to disappoint its following among
independent farmers. Clearly it hopes that continuing subsidy policies
focussed specifically on the rural poor will be sufficient to buy time.

It may, however, be the ultimate contradiction of Sri Lankan policy
that attempts to improve the position of the rural poor by radical measures
fail to receive the international support and indeed local support
that will produce faster modern sector growth while even half-successful
efforts at the latter almost automatically rule out success in the former.
We can conclude from this account that there are more conflicting interests
present in Sri Lanka than many observers realise and that successive
Governments have compromised between them. Welfare and subsidy programmes
have been a heaven-sent weapon in this respect. But we must doubt whether
fast growth and modernisation will themselves be sufficient to improve the
position of the rural poor without more forthright rural measures.

In the absence, however, of major changes there are some minor changes
which could usefully be undertaken in order to improve the position of the

poor. The first general issue concerns entitlement to ration books
allowing free or subsidised food and later, possibly, kerosene (although
charcoal for cooking fuel might be more useful). The income cut-off
point used to revalidate ration books in early 1978 implied a confiscatory
tax rate for incomes slightly above the limit. The exercise of assessing
income levels was undertaken quickly and inevitably inaccurately.[1]
Certain rules of thumb appear to have been used which discriminated against
those with a regular cash income, particularly, one feels, estate workers.
No account was taken of e.g. the greater food needs of estate women
labourers in lumping their household income together. So long as a range
of general subsidies, on wheat flour, on kerosene, still apply these
discriminatory effects are cushioned. In the future, however, the income
cut-off point may, literally, become a matter of life or death. We
therefore suggest that various benefits should not be given on an
"all-or-nothing" basis but that different levels should be given for
different groups. Furthermore income cannot be used as the dividing
line. An alternative ranking should be pursued based possibly on occupation
and land and other asset ownership. In this respect consideration should
be given to the populations most "at risk", e.g. encroachers and chena
cultivators on unirrigated lands where prolonged droughts are a major cause
of hardship, and village landless and marginal farmers who supplement their
incomes from insecure estate work.

Some similar remarks can be made in relation to the income support
scheme for the unemployed. This again revolves around a household income
figure (in fact using the same household information as that supplied for
ration book revalidation) and implies a high effective tax rate for households
just above the limit. However, the scheme does allow the unemployed to earn
up to Rs. 50 pm. without the household losing its entitlement to benefit.
The scheme can be criticised for excluding certain categories, e.g. married
persons, those under 18 and non-citizens. Our earlier analysis suggests
that the 18 year age limit may work against the poor.[2] Attention might
be given in the future to adding an "unemployment income support element"
to the benefits given through the ration.

---

[1] It seems fair to say that no-one, whether investigator or respondent,
can know a farmer's net income.

[2] Furthermore the 1978 list of eligible households is not to be revised in 1979, see Ministry of Plan Implementation, Employment data bank
and import support schemes, Colombo, 1979.

The distributional impact of the land reform programme needs to be throughly reviewed in order to grasp fully its potentials for employ ment, participation and local level planning. We would also like to suggest that the practice of drawing up farm plans with the active participation of members, and perhaps with the aid of the Agrarian Research and Training Institute, for land reform estates under Janawasas should be re-instated. This promises, once the corresponding investments are made, to be an effective means of assisting the young landless and near-landless workers.

One negative note we would like to sound concerns the possible establishment of a special agency for landless workers and marginal farmers. The problems of these groups do not seem to us susceptible to treatment of this nature. If small farmers rarely take institutional loans the kind of minor changes which a new agency might introduce are, we feel, very unlikely to assist them to do so. The problems are mixed in with tenancy, and being forced to take loans from landlords, and part-time farming. We would, however, like to see associations of landless workers and marginal farmers and perhaps also minimum wage legislation for rural workers inspite of their numerous implementational problems. Furthermore, it goes without saying, we would support fuller implementation of the Paddy Lands Act.